INDIA

THE LAST SUPERPOWER

INDIA
THE LAST SUPERPOWER

Hiroshi Hirabayashi

Translated from the Japanese by Prem Motwani

ALEPH

ALEPH BOOK COMPANY
An independent publishing firm
promoted by **Rupa Publications India**

First published in India in 2021
by Aleph Book Company
7/16 Ansari Road, Daryaganj
New Delhi 110 002

ISBN: 978-93-90652-34-1

1 3 5 7 9 10 8 6 4 2

Printed and bound in India by Parksons Graphics Pvt. Ltd.

CONTENTS

Prologue   vii

1. The Key to Understanding India   1

2. The Origins of Pro-Japan India   52

3. The Metamorphosis of India   109

4. Economic and Business Cooperation   133

5. How to Live and Work in India   163

Epilogue & Acknowledgements   197

PROLOGUE

India has emerged as a major power in Asia along with China in recent times. In the near future, India is projected to attain the status of the fourth global superpower to join the ranks of the United States of America, Russia, and China. No other country is expected to attain this status in the foreseeable future. Thus, India will remain the 'last' superpower for many generations.

India will overtake China in 2025 in terms of population

India's global profile is already gaining significance. Its importance in political, economic, cultural, and religious spheres has been steadily gaining ground. India has built cordial relations with the advanced nations of the West, including former colonial power, the United Kingdom, and communist Russia. In the last several decades, it has strived hard to strengthen relations with the United States of America and East Asia as the Asia–Pacific region has become the fulcrum of geopolitics in recent years.

At present, India's population stands at around 1.38 billion and is already the second largest in the world after China. It is expected to overtake China by the year 2025. At a time when several developed countries are experiencing serious demographic challenges with the increase of the elderly population, India enjoys a demographic advantage with a large young population leading to a healthy pyramid structure. In the education sector, India has also made considerable strides. By registering consistent high economic growth for some years, it now leads the group of emerging countries in the world.

India has risen to the rank of leading nations in the global comity of nations. India has the largest diaspora population in the world with around 13 million Indians living outside the country who have, in turn, contributed to India's global standing in considerable measure. As a result, India's influence on the international society has become noticeable.

Domestic reforms in India

The churning of India's domestic politics is quite rapid. The government of Prime Minister Narendra Modi is based on a strong foundation. This has enabled the government to put reforms on fast track.

With the aim to tackle black money in India, Prime Minister Modi unleashed a dramatic measure on 8 November 2016 to invalidate currency notes of two denominations—₹500 (about ¥800) and ₹1,000 (about ¥1,600) from midnight of the same day. This demonetization announcement took Indians and the whole world by surprise.

These two currency notes were of high denominations in India. These notes needed to be exchanged with the new ₹500 and ₹2,000 notes that were to be issued later. A period of some days were announced during which people could deposit the old notes in the banks and maintain the notes as legal tender, failing which such notes would be rendered useless.

There were two objectives behind this drastic measure. One was to make an attempt to curb the circulation of illegal money, corruption, and tender funding and the other was to counter the threat to the Indian law and order situation by the counterfeit currency used by terrorists.

The sudden decision to demonetize by the Modi government created panic in the whole country. There was a frenzied rush of people at banks and ATMs in an effort to withdraw cash. People overnight turned to payment gateways using credit cards. Corrupt businessmen, politicians, and bureaucrats were mere spectators as huge amounts of ill-gotten cash hoarded by them turned into mere pieces of waste paper. The ordinary citizens too faced severe hardships as the cash-based economy took a severe beating. But the move eventually worked wonders.

As a result, there was hardly any negative impact on the Indian economy. The Indian stock market (Sensex) remained unaffected and, in fact, surged sharply later.

In March 2017, state assembly elections were held in Uttar Pradesh (UP), the largest state in India. The Bharatiya Janata Party (BJP) registered a sweeping victory winning three-fourths of the seats. The inability of the regional parties to use black money for the elections also had its impact on the poll outcome. In other words, Modi's monetary policy seemed to have been endorsed by the people which encouraged Modi to further accelerate his economic reforms drive.

India's importance for Japan

India is an extremely important country for Japan. There are a variety of reasons for it, but the main ones are as follows:

- India is a leading pro-Japan country.
- India is the largest democracy in the world and its basic values are commonly shared with Japan.
- India is a leader amongst the developing nations and

at the same time has extremely good relations with America, Japan's ally.

- India is an important country for Japan, geopolitically as well as strategically.
- India's has huge economic potential and it is becoming increasingly important for the Japanese economy.

The Indian people place respect and faith in the Japanese people. The Indian government and Indian companies hold Japan in awe. Indians recognize Japan as a 'brother country' connected with spiritual bonds of Buddhism and basic values of democracy and freedom. As for the economy, India looks up to Japan as a mentor.

Pro-Japan India
What is the source of India's traditional pro-Japanese stance? I shall discuss about it in detail in Chapter 2, but let me briefly touch upon it here.

First of all, the bond of Buddhism is the foundation in this regard. Japan and India have historical and spiritual bonds based on Buddhism. Four heavenly kings or the eight legions such as Tathagata and Bodhisattva were originally Hindu divinities transmitted from India to Japan. This is evident if one visits Kofukuji National Treasure Hall in Nara or Toji and Sanjusangendo in Kyoto. Buddhist idols are displayed together with idols revered by Hindus in these famous Buddhist temples.

The biggest thing that Indians are grateful to Japan for is the latter's support and contribution towards India's independence movement.

The Japanese victory in the Russo–Japanese War (1904–05) inspired Indian freedom fighters. It was because Japan was the first Asian country to win against a mighty power, imperial Russia.

A small country, a dwarf, Japan, defeating a giant, Russia, not only enabled Japan to join the ranks of major powers, but this victory greatly impacted the rest of Asia. I had earlier talked to you about the excitement I had felt as a young man at the Japanese victories. This excitement was the same among all the men and women, young and old alike. A great European power had been defeated. Asia had scored a victory against Europe. Asian nationalism spread to the Eastern countries and cries of 'Asia for the Asians' were heard. A new Asian renaissance had begun, which showed hope for the future of Asia.

This was the essence of one of the letters Jawaharlal Nehru, the first prime minister of independent India, wrote to his daughter when he was imprisoned by the British colonial government. Nehru, who led the independence movement, is eloquently speaking here about how ecstatic he was at the Japanese victory in the Russo–Japanese War. These letters were later published under the title *Glimpses of World History*. The daughter was none other than Indira Gandhi who later went on to become prime minister of India.

Inspired by Japan's victory, freedom fighters seeking India's independence such as Rash Behari Bose came to Japan. Japanese volunteers extended willing support to them.

India's drive for independence was also spurred by the British surrender to the Japanese Army in Singapore and the establishment of the Indian National Army as well as the creation of the Provisional Government of Free India or simply, Azad Hind, by Subhas Chandra Bose.

India's relationship with post-war Japan
After the end of World War II, at the International Military Tribunal for the Far East (IMTFE) in Tokyo, a dissenting

judgement was written by an Indian judge, Radhabinod Pal, holding the trial invalid and exonerating the Japanese leaders of war crimes. The episode is well-known and it was not a mere coincidence. The main rationale behind it was the legal argument based on the principle of retrospective non-applicability of the international law, especially the criminal law. At the root, though, was also the high appreciation for Japan's support to India's independence and sympathy for a nation that had lost a war.

India did not join the San Francisco Peace Conference held on 8 September 1951. Prime Minister Nehru did not like its form, that is, victorious nations imposing unfair conditions on the defeated nation. A year later, in 1952, India signed a separate peace treaty with independent Japan and renounced its claim to war reparations.

During Japan's post-war reconstruction period, India was the first country to supply iron ore needed by Japan. India became the first recipient of Japan's Official Development Assistance (ODA) in 1956 which was used for the construction of a port in India.

There was then a hiatus in bilateral ties during the Cold War which saw the division of the world into two camps. During this period, while India advocated a policy of non-alignment, Japan was ensconced into the western camp. As a result of these ideological differences, both the countries drifted apart. When the Cold War ended in 1989 and the Soviet Union disintegrated thereafter, there was a dramatic turnaround. India was liberated from the Cold War mode of thinking and state-leading economy. With an emphasis to strengthen ties with the western nations as ordained by the market economy principle, its ties with Japan also gained a new momentum. In 1989, when Emperor Showa (Hirohito) of the Showa era

Hiroshi Hirabayashi

passed away, India declared national mourning, which was considered an exceptional gesture.

Rare friendship transcending the nuclear tests
In the 1990s, along with altering its erstwhile stance and attaching importance to its relations with western countries, India launched its 'Look East' policy. As India began to strive for domestic reforms, thereby registering high economic growth with aspiration to reach great power status, the distance between India and Japan started diminishing.

When India conducted nuclear tests in May 1998, India–Japan ties temporarily cooled off. Japan's reaction was quite sharp and one of disapproval. However, both countries soon made sincere efforts to improve bilateral relations. The author, who was the Japanese Ambassador to India at that time, requested the then Prime Minister Keizo Obuchi to visit India to restore cordial relations. Prime Minister Obuchi agreed but passed away suddenly. Yoshiro Mori who succeeded Obuchi agreed to the author's request to visit India.

Prime Minister Mori's visit to India in August 2000, after a gap of ten years by an incumbent Japanese prime minister, was a turning point in the evolution of India–Japan relations in recent times. Mori and his Indian counterpart, Prime Minister Atal Bihari Vajpayee, resolved to improve bilateral ties with all sincerity. Just after the summit meeting in New Delhi between the two prime ministers, 'Japan–India Global Partnership' was announced in order to clearly establish the global positioning of India and Japan that had moved to centre stage. It was upgraded to 'Strategic Global Partnership' in 2008 and further to 'Special Strategic Global Partnership' in 2014. Relationship in diverse areas such as foreign and security policy, economy, culture, science and technology, and personnel exchanges began to expand and strengthen subsequently.

This exceptional relationship is evidenced by the fact that the heads of governments of both countries not only meet in the global summits held across the world but the practice of visiting each other every alternate year has been established. Besides Russia, Japan is the only other country with which India has bilateral annual summits. This, in itself, is a rare relationship in the global context. For Japan, India is a trustworthy ally both politically and economically.

India enjoying high expectations from Japan

The Japan Bank for International Cooperation (JBIC), a quasi-governmental organization of Japan, conducts an annual survey by sending questionnaires to manufacturing companies of Japan to find out which countries are promising destinations for foreign investment in the medium-term. India has continued to be foremost among the promising investment destinations for the last three years. In the 2016 survey, 230 of the 483 companies (47.6 per cent) surveyed, put India at No. 1, China at No. 2 (203 companies, 42 per cent), Indonesia at No. 3 (173 companies, 35.8 per cent), Vietnam at No. 4 followed by Thailand, Mexico, America, the Philippines, Myanmar, and Brazil ranked at No. 10.

In addition, in the questionnaire-based survey (August 2016) targeting the digital version subscribers of the *Nihon Keizai Shimbun* (August 2016), known as the world's largest financial newspaper, the maximum number (56.1 per cent) of respondents in reply to the question: 'Which country in your opinion will grow the most in a few years?' chose India among the G20 countries.

Geopolitical importance
India is extremely important even in the geopolitical sense.

China has conflicts with Japan and Southeast Asia in the East China Sea and South China Sea respectively. It also has border conflicts with India in the Himalayan belt. In addition, China's advancement in the Indian Ocean in recent years has become increasingly conspicuous.

To counter this, Japan's cooperation and collaboration not only with leading nations of Southeast Asia such as the Philippines, Vietnam, Indonesia but also with India as a regional force, is indisputable. India too thinks along the same lines.

The Indian Ocean is covered by the jurisdiction of the US Seventh Fleet with its headquarters in Hawaii. Along with the Indian Navy, it safeguards the sea lanes passing through the Indian Ocean. These sea lanes are of vital importance for Japan too. Japan is fortunate that peace and safety of the Indian Ocean is being guaranteed by the US, its ally, as well as India, a country friendly with Japan. In recent times, these three countries—India, the United States, and Japan—have conducted annual joint navy exercises to ensure peace for safe maritime commerce.

JIA: Japan's oldest foreign friendship organization
I was posted in India as Japan's Ambassador to India for four years and eight months from March 1998. My posting was based on the recommendation of the then Prime Minister Ryutaro Hashimoto in whose government I had served as Chief Cabinet Councillor for Foreign Affairs (now renamed Assistant Chief Cabinet Secretary). Prime Minister Hashimoto also understood the geopolitical importance of India. He had remarked, 'If you become the ambassador in India, I

will definitely visit India as incumbent prime minister.' My contact with India until then was only through the channels of economic cooperation but complying with Hashimoto's wishes, I took up the post with a lot of hope and expectations. The ceremony for the presentation of the Japanese Emperor's credentials to the president of the Republic of India organized in April at Rashtrapati Bhavan was befitting a historically great nation and the ceremony itself was commendable. I shall give more details of this later.

Unfortunately, two months after I assumed office, India–Japan ties nosedived due to the 'nuclear tests' that India conducted in May 1998. Leading nations of the world, including Japan, protested against this and Japan resorted to sanctions such as suspension of the Official Development Assistance (ODA). As a gesture of protest, the Japanese government temporarily called the author back to Japan under the pretext of 'consultation with the home government'.

Normalcy was restored in India–Japan relations by 2000 after the visit of Prime Minister Yoshiro Mori to India. After this visit, bilateral relations continued to develop till the time the author completed his mission at the end of 2002 (details will be presented in Chapter 2). Prime Minister Mori is rightly seen both in India and Japan as the father of restoration of Indo–Japanese relations.

The author served as the Japanese Ambassador to France thereafter and retired in 2007 from active foreign service. And, as if by design, he was asked by Prime Minister Mori to join the Japan–India Association (JIA) as its president.

The Japan–India Association is the oldest friendship organization of Japan with any foreign country. It was established in 1903 by the elder statesman of Meiji, former Prime Minister Shigenobu Ohkuma, and the father of Japanese capitalism, Eiichi Shibusawa, and others. At that time India was a British colony. The Japan–Britain Society, a friendship organization with the colonial power of Great Britain, was established five years later in 1908. One can understand the foresight with which the founders of the JIA viewed the importance of India.

After resigning from the premiership, Mori succeeded Yoshio Sakurauchi, speaker of the House of Representatives of the Japanese Diet, as chairman of the JIA in 2003. The author, who felt indebted to Mori, accepted the offer extended to him willingly. Since then, the author's association with India, including the years he served as Japan's ambassador to India, amounts to more than fifteen years and is longer than that with France where he had served three terms as a diplomat for about eight years.

This book is being written and published with a view to sharing with as many people as possible such thoughts and precious experiences as the author had accumulated about India and the Japan–India relationship in the course of his professional engagement with India.

THE KEY TO UNDERSTANDING INDIA

India's relationship with Japan that saw a phase of estrangement after 1998 has seen a dramatic turnaround for the better. However, the understanding of the Japanese people about India is totally inadequate and seems to be flawed. Many Japanese are even prejudiced towards India. India and its people have depth in their national characters, which needs to be understood by the Japanese people. However, the perception of Indians towards Japan is different and is more of admiration. This book is aimed to remove some of the stereotypes that Japanese people harbour and elaborate on the varied facets of India in a way that would be easy to comprehend.

1.1 INDIA'S SIZE AND ECONOMIC STRENGTH

The first step to know India is to understand its size
India's total land mass is 3.28 million square kilometres. India is the seventh largest country in land mass in the world after Russia, Canada, the United States, China, Brazil, and Australia. Its size is almost the same as that of the European Union (EU). Japan's area is 378,000 square kilometres. Thus, India is about nine times bigger than Japan. The enormous geographical size

of India has led it to earn the epithet the 'Indian subcontinent'.

India has twenty-eight states and eight union territories. The European Union has twenty-eight member countries ranging from the Scandinavian countries to the Mediterranean countries. India and EU are similar in terms of size. When the Scandinavian countries are covered by snow, the Mediterranean countries experience a bright sun. The same is true of India. Even during the summer months, the Himalayan region and Kashmir region are covered with perennial snow. India's population, based on the 2011 Census, was put at 1.21 billion and today it is estimated to be 1.38 billion. Being the second largest country after China, India is projected to overtake China in population count by 2025. While China had imposed a one-child policy for many years, India does not have any such restriction.

As for population, in terms of youthfulness, India has the advantage. China largely has an ageing population whereas India's youth population is increasing. China's population composition is barrel type like Japan but India's is a perfect pyramid type. If seen economically, it is advantageous (called population bonus) as the working population is more. On the other hand, the population of Japan and China are feared to have negative impact on the economy due to population decline (called population onus).

However, it is not the labour force alone, but the enhancement of productivity based on technological innovation which is important for economic growth. The yardstick to measure growth based on population advantage alone can be flawed. There is no denying the fact, however, that the increase in young population, with other conditions being the same, is an advantage for India.

Moreover, the size of the middle class in India is growing

rapidly. Though the definition of the middle class varies from person to person, according to the author, it is those who earn between ₹200,000 to ₹2 million per annum. Such population is increasing at a rate of 20 million every year. The sustained high economic growth has led the middle class to move to higher income bracket and the poor class to move to the middle income bracket, reflecting in the steady increase in the per capita income of people. According to the World Bank, India's per capita income was reported at US$2,104 in 2019.

If seen in terms of Purchasing Power Parity (PPP), India ranks third in the world after China and the United States.

With the growth of economic power, education levels too have improved, leading to the rise in the literacy rate. According to the 2011 Census, the literacy rate in India was 74 per cent. Since it was 65 per cent at the time of the 2001 Census, in ten years it has improved by ten percentage points. While the economic divide in India is wide depending on the region, even the literacy rate varies considerably from region to region. In 2020, data shows that in the state of Bihar, literacy rate is low at 70.9 per cent but in the state of Kerala it is 96.2 per cent. In short, India is not only big in terms of size, but it is also improving qualitatively quite rapidly. There is thus a need to correct the stereotyped view of India as a poor developing country.

1.2 WORLD'S LARGEST DEMOCRACY

Common greetings exchanged between Americans and Indians
There is a common greeting that Indians and Americans often exchange between them. Indians applaud America as 'the oldest democracy in the world' and Americans return the gesture by saying 'India is the largest democracy in the world'.

Why is India the 'world's largest democracy'?

The Indian electorate number was estimated at 814 million (at the time of the general elections in 2014), which was the largest in the world.

In India, men and women above eighteen years of age have the voting right. The general elections for the Lok Sabha or the Lower House of the Parliament (its term is five years but it can be dissolved and the number of seats is currently 543) have the largest electorate in the world.

Conducting elections is a tough job in India. Lok Sabha elections held in 2014 were conducted over five weeks in nine phases. In large states, elections are conducted over seven to nine days, the reason being deployment of officials and police for the management of elections, and law and order measures to secure voting places.

In the spring of 2017, during elections for the state legislative assembly of Uttar Pradesh, which has the largest population in India, elections were conducted over seven days.

Elections to the parliament and state legislative assemblies are administered by the Election Commission, an autonomous constitutional body which performs its mission and responsibility immaculately. It enjoys absolute powers with respect to deciding the election schedule, supervision of election campaigning, supervision of voting and finalization of voting schedule, certification of election irregularities, and so on. When it announces the election results, no one challenges its authority and credibility. Interestingly, the Election Commission comprises just three members.

Why is United States the 'oldest democracy' in the world?

Ever since the United States declared its independence following its victory in the war with Great Britain, it has adopted the democratic system. The Declaration of Independence officially adopted on 4 July 1776, boasts of being the oldest document that laid down the principles of the republic system and democracy. Therefore, it is called the 'oldest democracy' in the world.

The Declaration of Independence was a declarative statement announcing independence from Great Britain. Its introductory words are as follows:

> We hold these truths to be self-evident, that all Men are created equal, that they are endowed by their Creator with certain unalienable Rights, that among these are Life, Liberty and the pursuit of Happiness. That to secure these rights, Governments are instituted among Men, deriving their just powers from the Consent of the Governed, That whenever any form of Government becomes destructive of these Ends, it is the Right of the People to alter or to abolish it, and to institute new Government, laying its Foundation on such Principles and organizing its Powers in such form, as to them shall seem most likely to affect their Safety and Happiness.

The independence of India and the United States is nearly three centuries apart but they are common in terms of having gained independence from the shackles of the British empire and find resonance with each other.

Light and shade of Indian democracy

According to the author, democracy has two facets. One is the substantive (or the content) front and the other is the procedural front.

India adopted the democratic system after Independence. The Constituent Assembly formed for drafting and finalizing the Constitution of India first met on 9 December 1946. There were representatives from each religious community and caste, including the lowest Scheduled Castes (the so-called outcastes), Christians, Muslims, Sikhs, Parsis, and Buddhists.

India's Constitution was promulgated on 26 January 1950 when free India declared itself a republic. This date is now celebrated as the Republic Day.

The Indian Constitution stipulates various principles of democracy such as equality of all citizens, justice, liberty, fundamental human rights, fraternity to maintain unity of the nation, and so on. However, India is faced with many problems such as economic disparity, lack of equal opportunity in education, abuse of power, and so on. Particularly, although the caste system is unconstitutional and illegal, it still exists as social custom and stigma, contrary to the spirit of democracy.

On the procedural front, though, democracy is functional in India. The Centre and the states are always administered respectively by governments directly elected through elections. India has experienced neither a coup nor a military regime since Independence. It can be called a rare instance among developing countries. The only blemish could be the declaration of a country-wide Emergency by Prime Minister Indira Gandhi, the daughter of the first prime minister of India, Jawaharlal Nehru. In the general elections conducted in 1971, the Indian National Congress led by Indira Gandhi was accused of electoral violations and the High Court pronounced her guilty and declared the elections null and void. Indira Gandhi opposed it and declared the Emergency, and over a period of seven months she restricted various rights of people (freedom of expression, assembly, and association), introduced censorship, and arrested her opponents. She lifted the Emergency in 1977, being confident that she would win the general elections if held at that time. However, she had to face defeat in the elections. India's electorate rejected her as she had tampered with democracy.

In India, which has adopted a parliamentary cabinet system similar to the one in the United Kingdom and Japan, the head of the largest party in the Lok Sabha is normally chosen as the leader of the Lok Sabha and is invited by the president to form the government.

The pillars of Indian democracy

Indian democracy is respected and maintained through several supporting pillars and political culture.

First is the enthusiasm of the people to actively participate in elections which is reflected in the high voting rate of the electorate. The Parliament of India is a bicameral legislature. The Lower House or the Lok Sabha (House of the People), has 545 members (two Anglo–Indian members are nominated by the president) with a term of five years. The members of the Lok Sabha are directly elected by the people. The Upper House or the Rajya Sabha (Council of States), has 250 members with a term of six years. Its members are indirectly elected. The elected members of the Parliament and legislative assemblies of the states are eligible to vote and elect the members of the Rajya Sabha.

There are many political parties in India. Besides the national parties such as the Indian National Congress (INC), Bharatiya Janata Party BJP), and Communist Party of India (CPI), among others, there are regional parties having their political bases in their respective states.

Some regional parties are strongly rooted in respective states where they enjoy suzerainty, and national parties, at times, find it difficult to grab power there. Regional parties accord more priority to the interests of their respective states even if they enter the arena of national politics.

After the one-party domination by the Congress ended, the coalition era began. Presently, it is the BJP-led coalition known as the National Democratic Alliance (NDA) which is at the Centre.

During elections, political parties deploy buses and trucks to bring voters to the voting booths. The underprivileged segments of the electorate keep high hopes on the elections to elect leaders of their choice who, they hope, will free them from poverty and social discrimination. However, more often than not, once elected to power, governments often fail to fulfil their election promises. As a result, the expectations of the people are often not met. The party/parties in power fail to keep their commitments either because of the serious nature of problems, corruption, or conflict of vested interests reflecting the complexity of the Indian society and politics.

In such cases, the electorates opt for a change of government in the next election by outvoting the party in power. Such a phenomenon is seen both at the Centre and the states when elections are held. In certain states, the electorate frequently forms or supports the party that represents their caste. This is called 'caste politics'. For example, at one time, the Samajwadi Party (SP) that represents the interests of the backward castes, and the Bahujan Samaj Party (BSP) that largely represents the Scheduled Castes alternately came to power in Uttar Pradesh. However, in the state elections held in 2017, the BJP secured 312 seats out of 403, and the regional parties were relegated to a minority status.

The second pillar of Indian democracy is the mass media. In India, the mass media, both electronic and print, are quite vibrant. They scrutinize the performance of the government fearlessly. In a multilingual country, with electronic and print media in many regional languages, the figures in terms of circulation are staggering. The qualitative standard of reporting and coverage is also quite high. Indian mass media is free, independent, and transparent and works as a watchdog in a democratic country. They do not pander to power. Indian mass media can be seen as similar to British and American media.

The third pillar is the judiciary. For the entire nation, there is one unified judicial system. The Supreme Court of India is the top court and the last appellate court in India. It is also the arbiter in matters of relations between the union and the states and between the states. India's judicial system is similar to that in Japan. The professional standard of Indian judges is quite high, and the quality and integrity of the Supreme Court judges are at par with their counterparts in the advanced nations. Justice Radhabinod Pal of India, who sat on the bench as one of the three Asian judges appointed to the International Military Tribunal for the Far East in Tokyo, and delivered an impressive minority opinion against the judgement, which accused Japan and 'war criminals' of being guilty, had the honour of serving as a judge in the Calcutta High Court.

In India, the Central Bureau of Investigation (CBI), similar to the FBI in the United States, enjoys considerable authority, and yet if the CBI is unable to take action or is seen to slacken, at times, the Supreme Court has had to order the investigating body to conduct or expedite enquiry in certain cases. Being the highest court of the country, its decisions are binding not only for the government but also for all civilians.

The fourth pillar is the armed forces. The Indian armed forces are the military forces of India. The president of India serves as the supreme commander of the Indian armed forces. The armed forces consist of the Indian Army, Indian Air

Force, and Indian Navy and are under the Ministry of Defence of the Government of India. In such a structure, the division of power is clearly defined by the Constitution and practised. According to the author's experience, the chiefs of the Indian armed forces are men with the highest levels of integrity, bravery, courage, and loyalty.

1.3 UNITY IN DIVERSITY

Systems that secure unity

It was Prime Minister Jawaharlal Nehru who first used the term 'unity in diversity'. This term denotes India's unified plurality even today. India is extremely diverse in terms of race, language, history, culture, and regional ethos. But as a country it is one entity and remains united. This diversity is a unique feature of the country and attracts a lot of global attention.

There are several ingenuous ways through which India secures its unity in diversity. First, is the system of bureaucracy. The Indian bureaucratic system has its origins in the British era. One needs to be an Indian Administrative Service (IAS) officer to become a bureaucrat. The civil services examination is known to be an extremely difficult national level competitive exam and if one joins this elite group, one has the power to do a lot for his/her country. It is similar to the higher civil services exam held in Japan in the pre-war years. In present-day Japan, if one clears the advanced level of civil services examination, he/she joins the select band of elite bureaucracy commonly referred to as 'career bureaucrat'. However, Japan's pre-war civil services officers and India's present-day IAS officers are much more elite in nature than the present-day career bureaucrats in Japan. As elite bureaucrats, there are also the

Indian Foreign Service (IFS) officers who are of the same rank as the IAS. The system is already abolished in Japan but is equivalent to those who had passed the erstwhile Advance Diplomat Exam.

The salient feature of the IAS is the posting in each state of those who have successfully qualified. Posting in a particular state is called 'cadre allocation'. The state of posting is decided depending on the concerned person's choice of state and rank of the candidate in the final merit list. An influential politician could also play a part in the cadre allocation of a particular candidate. Big states like UP that have a big impact on Indian politics are highly competitive. Once the state cadre allocation is decided, IAS officers climb up the career ladder while shuffling between central ministries and the respective state government to which they are attached. When they are assigned to a state, they occupy key positions and their designations and responsibilities are higher than they have at a central ministry. For instance, a joint secretary of the Ministry of Commerce and Industry, becomes secretary, Ministry of Commerce and Industry at the state level. This is quite similar in Japan where a bureaucrat of the Ministry of Internal Affairs and Communication, for example, gets a higher position when deputed to one of the forty-seven prefectures in Japan.

Another feature of the IAS is that even if IAS officers are in a central ministry, they are not attached exclusively to one ministry but could be reshuffled with other ministries of the government depending on their domain expertise. This depends on the wish of the minister concerned and also on the willingness of the concerned IAS officer. In other words, the IAS officers often act as a link between the central and state governments.

Another system that ensures unity of the country is the governors who are appointed by the president of India. The governor is the chief executive head of the state and works as the representative of the central government. But like the president of India, the governor is a nominal head in the state. At present, there are twenty-eight state governors and eight administrators/lieutenant governors (LG) of union territories.

A governor's role in a state is almost ceremonial. He/she has no substantive role to perform as long as state politics are functioning normally. During normal times, a governor is usually invited as the chief guest to various functions, and yet his/her job is, at best, to deliver a speech. However, when state politics are under turmoil, and the state passes through political instability, the governor, as the president's representative in the state, has to act. And it is not rare in India for state politics to be in a crisis. When there is a political crisis, and no political party enjoys the confidence to form the state government, the governor mostly advises the Centre to impose President's Rule in the state. Until political normalcy is restored, or another election takes place, the governor rules the state as the representative of the president. During this period of President's Rule, all political powers to govern the state are vested with the governor on behalf of the president. Once normalcy is restored, the power of governance is returned to a newly elected state government headed by a chief minister.

This demonstrates that the role of the governor is that of a representative of the president and is higher in terms of protocol than that of the administrative head in the state or the chief minister who is directly elected through an election. During his posting in India, the author invariably made a courtesy call to both the governor and the chief minister whenever he visited a particular state. Raj Bhavan is the common name of the official residences of governors of states. The official residence of a governor is rarely located in the heart of the state capital and is usually situated in a picturesque location.

This system to have both the appointed governor and the directly elected chief minister in the state is exactly the same as that in France. The difference in their rank and authority is almost the same. In France, there are departments that are equivalent to Indian states and regions that have several departments combined together. Both the department and the region have respectively their own governor (called prefect in France) appointed by the Centre and the administrative head (president of the council) elected directly by the electorate.

Ethnic diversity

Dravidians, supposedly the first race to have settled in the subcontinent, Aryans, who are thought to have entered later from Central Asia, and the Mongoloids who conquered and later inhabited parts of the Northeast are the main races of India. Over time, India's ethnic composition has become quite complex due to repeated intermingling.

North Indians are primarily of Aryan origin while South Indians are mostly of Dravidian origin. As is obvious from the term 'Indo–Aryan' race, the facial features and build of Aryans are similar to that of Europeans and Iranians. Their complexion is also comparatively fair but due to the intense heat of the sun in India and mixing of blood over centuries, many now have darker complexions. On the other hand, there are women with blue eyes in the north such as in Kashmir.

Here, let me digress a little. India boasts of being the most prolific film-making nation in the world. The number of films made easily exceeds 800 in a year. India produces films not only in Hindi but in all the major Indian languages. The majority of heroes and heroines look to be of Aryan origin and are fair complexioned. They dance to the fast rhythm of Indian music. The unique nature of Bollywood films (coined by combining Bombay and Hollywood) is to have plenty of beautiful dance scenes, though that may have nothing to do with the main plot. Besides Mumbai (formerly Bombay), Chennai (formerly Madras), and Hyderabad, there are other centres of film-making in India. There are many actors and actresses who have also turned politicians.

When the author was posted here, India won three world beauty contests in one year; Miss Universe, Miss International, and Miss Photogenic. Indian's pride was at its peak at that time. All the three women were Aryan-looking and fair complexioned.

Linguistic diversity

India is extremely diverse in languages. According to the Constitution of India, Hindi is the official language of the country and English is an associate official language. But there are around twenty-two languages that are also treated as official languages or schedule languages. The Hindi-speaking population is the largest but it still accounts for only around 43 per cent of the population. The only language used at a pan-India level is English—the language of the former colonial power, Great Britain. It is mainly the middle class and the upper class who can use the English language in most parts of India.

Large states have their official languages used in the state.

Punjabi in Punjab, Marathi in Maharashtra, Bengali in West Bengal, Tamil in Tamil Nadu, Odia in Odisha, Kannada in Karnataka, Malayalam in Kerala, and so on. The scripts of North Indian and South Indian languages are completely different. To put it more simply, the script of North Indian languages comes mostly from Sanskrit and is similar to the Japanese Katakana, whereas that of the South Indian languages is similar to the Japanese Hiragana.

In the Indian Parliament, there are members who use earphones to avail of simultaneous interpretation facility. Among them there are many who cannot speak either English or Hindi. They speak only in their regional languages. It is similar to the European Parliament. Even in the European Parliament that is located in Strasbourg in France near the German border, simultaneous interpretation is used as members belong to different countries in Europe.

On the reverse side of India's currency notes besides the numerals, its denomination is written in Hindi and English. It is for the convenience of people but reflects the linguistic diversity of India.

Diverse languages

Hindi is the official language and is spoken by over 43 per cent of the population according to the 2011 Census. There are 121 languages which are spoken by 10,000 or more people in India. The Indian Constitution recognizes twenty-two languages as official languages. As a symbol of linguistic diversity, fifteen of the twenty-two languages are written on the panel which appear on the reverse of the note displaying the denomination of the note. The languages are Assamese, Bengali, Gujarati, Kannada, Kashmiri, Konkani, Malayalam, Marathi, Nepali, Odia, Punjabi, Sanskrit, Tamil, Telugu, and Urdu.

SPEECH IN THE LOCAL LANGUAGE

In India, English is usually spoken at the place of work and, hence, language is not a problem. However, due to laziness, the author did not make an effort to study the Hindi language. However, he had to travel to various places for work and deliver speeches or make opening remarks at various functions. Hence, he could not have been indifferent to the languages. In order to earn the goodwill and the attention of the audience, he made an effort to greet people at the beginning for a brief while in the local language. After the initial remark he would say, 'My skill in the local language does not allow me to go beyond this in the local language' and used to quickly switch to English. The audience would cheer him because they could understand that the author had respected the local language, history, and culture.

The author would request his secretary to pronounce the text in Hindi and made notes in Katakana and intonated it in Hindi style and practised pronouncing it. Even with such a superficial approach he could communicate well in Hindi. However, South Indian languages, for instance, Tamil and Kannada (although both have somewhat similar characters and pronunciation) were difficult to pronounce. He found it difficult to convert them easily into Katakana and had a tough time.

◆

Religious diversity: history of confrontation and coexistence

India is a department store of religions

India's diversity is particularly notable in terms of religion.

India witnessed the birth of four religions between the ancient and medieval ages. They are Brahmanism (considered to be the predecessor of Hinduism), Buddhism, Jainism, and Sikhism. India also has other religious faiths such as Christianity, Judaism, Islam, and Zoroastrianism.

According to the 2011 Census, 79.8 per cent of Indians were Hindus, 14.2 per cent Muslims, 2.3 per cent Christians, 1.7 per cent Sikhs, 0.7 per cent Buddhists, 0.4 per cent Jains, and over 60,000 who practised Zoroastrianism.

By the way, the Indian national flag has saffron, white, and green colour bands. Saffron symbolizes courage and sacrifice, green symbolizes faith and chivalry, white symbolizes honesty, peace, and purity and the Ashoka Chakra rendered in navy blue against the white background signifies that there is life in movement and death in stagnation.

Religious history full of vicissitudes

Hinduism

Hinduism and Brahmanism, its predecessor, are polytheistic, meaning worshipping multiple gods, like Shintoism in Japan. Brahmanism was born around 1000 BCE when the Indo–Aryans entered India through the Indus Valley in the north-west. In the process of establishing their domination while intermingling with the Dravidians, the primitive religious thoughts that they brought with them got blended with local religious thoughts. With the passage of time, the form and content of faith got streamlined and refined and it was theorized in the form of the Vedas.

Many gods and goddesses appear in Indian mythology. For example, Indra is the god of thunder, Agni the god of fire, and Surya is the sun god. Tales (legends) of these divinities are extremely interesting. The teachings of Brahmanism are interspersed in these tales to communicate them to the masses in an attractive manner. Mahabharata (meaning Great India) and Ramayana (the tale of Prince Ram) are two grand epics, full of the teachings of Brahmanism. It is similar to Japan's *Kojiki*, the first Japanese literature depicting the legends of Shintoism and gods and goddess followed by epics of the emperors of Japan from the first Emperor Jimmu (the legendary fifth descendant of Sun Goddess Amaterasu, creator of Japan) to the thirty-third Emperor Suiko (554–628 CE).

As described later, Brahmanism was substituted gradually by Buddhism that emerged as a reformative religion with increasing popularity. In spite of the popular nature of Buddhism, after the third century, in Indian dynasties, Brahmanism continued to survive as a popular faith and eventually transformed itself into Hinduism. It is believed that Islam entered India from the north as early as the seventh century. Then, from the early sixteenth century, the Mughal empire dominated more than half of India, and yet Hinduism survived as the popular faith.

There are three important gods in the Hindu pantheon: Lord Brahma, the creator of the universe; Lord Vishnu, the preserver of the universe; and Lord Shiva who destroys the universe once it has degenerated and then passes it on to Lord Brahma for fresh creation of the universe.

From left to right: Lord Brahma, Early Chola Dynasty, Tenth Century, South India; Lord Vishnu, Pala Dynasty, Eleventh Century, East India; Lord Shiva, Konarak, Thirteenth Century, East India. All these statues are displayed at the National Archaeological Museum, Delhi. Photos courtesy of the author.

Hiroshi Hirabayashi

Since Lord Brahma is regarded as an abstract and philosophical God, he is less accessible for mortals. There are dedicated temples for worshipping Lord Brahma such as in Pushkar in Rajasthan, but their number is very small. Therefore, popular faith gets directed to Lord Vishnu or Lord Shiva. Since Lord Shiva is a frightening god, his popularity is partly out of fear and partly out of awe.

It is important to note that in Hinduism it is believed that Buddha who founded Buddhism was the ninth incarnation of Lord Vishnu who had come to rescue this world from degeneration. According to Hindu mythology, Lord Vishnu reincarnates (avatar) and appears on the earth whenever the world is exposed to the threat of evil or is under turmoil and rescues it each time. So far he is believed to have appeared in nine avatars and there will be the tenth avatar called Kalki who will save the world from evil.

The first avatar was Matsya—depicted as a huge fish or as a human torso connected to the tail of a fish, second was Kurma, a giant tortoise, third was Varaha, a boar, fourth was Narasimha, in the form of half-man and half-lion, fifth was Vamana, a dwarf, sixth was Parashurama, the saint with an axe, seventh was Rama, the central figure of the epic Ramayana, eighth was Balarama or Krishna, the divine statesman of the Mahabharata, the ninth avatar is Buddha, and the tenth will be Kalki, with Lord Vishnu appearing on a white horse with a mighty sword in the present Kali Yuga.

If we see the sequence of these avatars, they are fish (although half-man), tortoise (amphibian), boar (mammal), man (mankind), and gods. Their sequence follows the order of Darwin's theory of evolution, except the gods. Did ancient Indians have an understanding of the evolution of animals long before Darwin whose book *The Origin of Species* was written in the nineteenth century?

The explanation for this is paradoxical. The legend says that the world was threatened when demons appeared to inhabit it. Therefore, Lord Vishnu reincarnated as Buddha and preached Buddhism to the demons, so that demons deviated from Brahmanism and Vedic teachings and eventually lost their power. Thus, the Hindu world was rescued. Here, Buddhism is not regarded as a rightful religion in itself but interpreted as a religion that deviated from the right course to protect Brahmanism and then Hinduism. This paradoxical interpretation may derive from a Hindu centrism.

It is believed that in the distant future when the world reaches its end (Kalyug), the tenth reincarnation of Lord Vishnu will emerge riding a white horse. It is called Kalki. And if the universe is in a chaotic stage beyond the control of Kalki, it will be the time for Lord Shiva, the god of destruction, to appear. Lord Shiva will destroy the universe and will leave it for Lord Brahma to recreate the universe again. Interestingly, here the universe itself is the object of reincarnation—metempsychosis.

As described later, Hindu divinities were introduced in Japan along with Buddhism. Lord Brahma as Bonten, Lord Vishnu as Bichuten or Naraenten, Shiva as Daijizaiten or Daikokuten. Only some attributes of each one of them were introduced but if seen from the perspective of Hindus, it was an awesome development.

Buddhism

Brahmanism degenerated into a mere shell with time while caste-based discrimination also took root. Thereupon, Buddhism and Jainism emerged as reformist movements. As such, both were reformative religions that attempted to reform the negative aspects of Brahmanism and recreate religions that were easier to comprehend for people. Both religions were born in India in the fifth and sixth centuries.

Buddhism was founded by Prince Siddhartha Gautama of the Shakya clan, and Jainism by Mahavira of the Magadh kingdom. There are various theories about the time of birth of Siddhartha Gautama. Professor Hajime Nakamura, a Japanese authority on Indian philosophy and Buddhism, estimated it at around 463 BCE. Siddhartha was a prince of the kingdom of the Shakya clan. One day when he went out of the palace, he was exposed to the problems of Brahmanism and the sufferings of humanity. He shunned his position and left his palace, seeking salvation. He did penance for long but could not achieve enlightenment. He was reduced to a thin frame of skin and bones and reached Niranjana River. Sujata, a milkmaid, seeing his plight, offered him rice and milk. Siddhartha, who was on the verge of starvation, got some reprieve by eating what he was offered and reached a bodhi tree. It was in present-day Bodh Gaya. He meditated for forty-nine days under the tree and finally attained enlightenment. It was the birth of Buddha (one who has attained bodhi or wisdom or who has awakened to truth). That is why he is also called Shakyamuni.

The big bodhi tree is actually located in present-day Bodh Gaya at the foot of a tall tower in the Mahabodhi Temple premises which is a UNESCO World Heritage Site. According to the resident priest, who showed the author around when he visited the temple, it is a grafted tree and the fourth generation descendant of the original bodhi tree. But the authenticity of it is yet to be checked. Buddhist believers from various places were going around the tower clockwise and were offering their prayers by prostrating repeatedly.

After attaining enlightenment, Lord Buddha headed westwards and reached Sarnath. Buddha held his first sermon there before his five disciples. Deer from the surrounding forest also gathered to hear his sermon. In the very place where Lord Buddha held his first sermon now stands the remains of the massive Dhamek Stupa.

Thereafter, until his death around forty-five years later, Buddha continued to spread his teachings in present-day Bihar and Uttar Pradesh along with his disciples who continued to increase in numbers. He stayed the longest in Rajagriha (present-day Rajgir in Bihar. Rajgir means house of the king). Buddha repeated his daily sermons and meditation, travelling between the bamboo grove, abode offered to him by King Bimbisara of Magadh, and Gridhakuta (Mount Ryojusen). And he developed his religious community. The author, while travelling around Buddhist heritage sites, climbed Mount Ryojusen with his wife early in the morning. There are Buddhist relics on top of this mountain, and even the stone on which Lord Buddha is believed to have preached is still intact. Seeing the red morning sun rising from the east, the author slipped into a feeling of devotion and awe.

Major Buddhist heritages are spread from Bihar to Lumbini (in present-day Nepal). Lumbini, Bodh Gaya, Sarnath, and Kushinagar (where Buddha attained nirvana) are considered the four holiest places of Buddhism. There are four other holy places and are collectively called the eight holy places of Buddhism. The other four are Rajagriha, Sahet–Mahet (Jetavana Vihar and the headquarters of his religious community), Vaishali (the last place of sermon) and Sankassa, place of ascension to heaven. Except for the last one, all the other holy places actually exist.

Lord Buddha's last journey ended in Kushinagar in present-day Uttar Pradesh. Buddha developed fever and passed away surrounded by his disciples. He finally attained nirvana.

He was cremated there and his ashes were divided into eight portions and were handed over to the kings and people of influence. Stupas were constructed to enshrine the ashes of Lord Buddha. As described later, Emperor Ashoka of the Maurya empire further minutely divided Lord Buddha's ashes into 80,000 portions of bones, teeth, ashes, and so on, as there were many who wanted a part of Buddha's body. Thus Lord Buddha's ashes reached not only different parts of India but eventually distant countries such as China, Japan, Sri Lanka, Myanmar, and Thailand. The author was shown a small piece of bone excavated at Vaishali, thanks to the generous local head of the Archaeological Survey of India. The author was told that researchers of the Archaeological Survey of India had confirmed after appraisal that it was, in fact, an authentic part of Lord Buddha's body. The author could not believe it at first, but seeing the relics of the stupa nearby, was finally convinced about its authenticity.

Buddhism spread across the Indian subcontinent and further to East Asia (Mahayana Buddhism) and to Southeast Asia (Theravada or Hinayana Buddhism) and became a global religion.

In the third century, the Maurya dynasty in North India expanded its territory by conquering neighbouring kingdoms. Emperor Ashoka, third generation ruler of the Maurya dynasty, expanded his empire through military strength. Around 265 BCE, he defeated the powerful Kalinga kingdom that ruled the present-day Odisha state in the Kalinga War. However, hundreds of thousands of soldiers and others perished during the battle on both sides, and the land and the river turned red with blood. Emperor Ashoka deeply repented it and embraced Buddhism. Emperor Ashoka's control stretched over a vast swathe of land across India. He used the teachings of Buddhism in order to be a good ruler.

Even today one finds Ashoka pillars in many places that he had conquered. Delhi has two of them. The Ashoka pillar at Sarnath has four lions standing back to back and a graphic representation of it was adopted as the national emblem of India.

The four lions mounted on top of a lotus flower in full bloom symbolize power, courage, confidence, and pride. All government buildings in India invariably have this emblem on their front and all official documents also carry it.

Buddhism spread across the whole of India as Emperor Ashoka endeavoured to conduct politics based on Buddhism and dharma. Emperor Ashoka sent one of his princes thought to be either his son or younger brother to Sri Lanka to introduce Buddhism. From there Buddhism developed into Theravada (Hinayana Buddhism) that got popular in Southeast Asia. Incidentally, Sri Lanka is considered to be the island ruled by Ravana, who had kidnapped and held Sita captive, the wife of Prince Rama, in the Ramayana.

Along with Buddhism spreading across the world, Buddhist art flourished in various parts of India and beyond.

Formerly, the northern part of Southeast Asia belonged to the Chinese cultural sphere and the southern part was within the Indian cultural sphere. Theravada (it is popularly called Hinayana as against Mahayana that was introduced in China and Japan via Northwest India) Buddhism travelled to Southeast Asia from South India. Today, the religion practised in Thailand and Cambodia may be described as a mixture of Buddhism and Hinduism.

Jainism

Jainism was founded by a philosopher, Nigantha Nataputta, around the same time and in the same region of Bihar as Buddhism. He was called Mahavira and after penance he attained supreme wisdom. Both Buddhism and Jainism are quite similar in philosophy, but while Buddhism is a gentle religion, Jainism has very strict tenets and is quite rigid about what is clean and what is unclean. It is for this rigidity that it did not spread widely and was confined mainly to northern and western India.

Islam

Islam originated in the Arabian Peninsula in the seventh century and spread both to the East and West. It entered the Indian subcontinent also through land and sea routes. North India had rivalry among the Rajput (kshatriya class in Hinduism) clans between the seventh and tenth centuries. Islam spread its power in northern India. In the twelfth century, Islamic sultans entered India from the north-west, fought with the Rajputs, gradually subjugated them, and established their supremacy over the region surrounding Delhi. Five Islamic dynasties with different sultans at the helm ruled from the Mamluk dynasty to the Lodi dynasty. They are collectively called the Delhi Sultanate.

In the sixteenth century, a different Islamic power led by Babur from Timur's lineage entered India from Central Asia, conquered the Lodi dynasty, and established the Mughal empire in 1526. The Mughal empire's territory was the largest during the reign of the sixth ruler, Emperor Aurangzeb, and thus Islam spread as far as the Deccan Plateau in central India.

In an India dominated by Islam, Buddhism was driven to the Himalayas and Jainism remained alive in Rajasthan and

Gujarat. Hinduism survived as a popular faith.

And in western and southern India where the Mughals could not dominate, various Hindu princely states held their ground and the situation was like the fiefs of the daimyos in the feudal Edo period of Japan.

With the British dominance becoming strong, the Mughal empire declined. Princely states and their maharajas gradually succumbed to the British.

In 1858, Bahadur Shah Zafar, the last Mughal emperor, was driven away to Burma (present-day Myanmar) resulting in the collapse of the Mughal empire.

Sikhism

Sikhism was born as a result of conflicts between Hindus and Muslims. Sikhism was founded by Guru Nanak (1469–1539) in Punjab in Northwest India between the fifteenth and sixteenth centuries.

Guru Nanak criticized both Hinduism and Islam for their façade and preoccupation with rituals and customary practices. He rejected rituals, idol worship, penance, the caste system, and superstitions. In short, Sikhism is believed to have got rid of the 'bad aspects' of Hinduism and Islam and retained the good aspects. Sikhism believes that there is only one God and that the name of God only differs from religion to religion. On the other hand, it retained the concept of reincarnation of Hinduism and Buddhism.

After Guru Nanak, there were nine Gurus and the tenth was Guru Gobind Singh (1666–1708). After him the spirit of the Guru transferred itself to the sacred scripture of Sikhism, the Guru Granth Sahib.

Males in Sikhism wear a unique turban. The Japanese image of Indian males is that of strong men wearing turbans.

That image comes from the Sikhs. They never remove their turban in front of others. It is said that they keep a weapon besides a comb inside the turban. Sikhs were persecuted by Islamists and Hindus since the beginning and it is because of this that they have a long history of fighting. Hindus and Muslims in Rajasthan and Gujarat wear a turban but its shape is different from that of the Sikhs.

Christianity

It is said that Christianity was introduced here when the Portuguese entered India during the Age of Exploration. There is a legend that one of the Twelve Apostles of Christianity, Saint Thomas, had come to India during the first century for missionary work. A cave where Saint Thomas is said to have meditated is located on top of a hill near the airport of Chennai and Saint Thomas Church where his mortal remains are buried is located in the city.

If one talks of Christianity in India, one cannot avoid referring to Saint Francis Xavier. Full-scale missionary work to spread Christianity in India was started with the dedicated efforts of the Society of Jesus. It was a missionary organization established by Ignatius of Loyola and Francis Xavier, aristocrats from the Basque country in north-west Spain in the sixteenth century. They had graduated from the University of Paris (Sorbonne) and got permission from the Pope to do missionary work. The Portuguese king dispatched Xavier to Goa on the west Indian shore. Xavier reached Goa in 1542 and he went for missionary work to Malacca in the Malay Peninsula in 1545, and Moluccas Islands in 1546. When he returned to Malacca in 1547, he met the Japanese Yasujiro (Anjiro) who had been converted to Christianity and he came up to Japan with him. Xavier first entered Kagoshima in southern Kyushu and met provincial military governor turned daimyo (equivalent to maharaja) Takahisa Shimazu. Next, he went to Hirado in Hizen, western Kyushu, and then to Yamaguchi in Suo, western mainland Honshu, and met Daimyo Ouchi Yoshitaka. He proceeded to the capital Kyoto to meet the monarch of Japan (at that time it was Emperor Go-Nara) to seek permission for missionary work in Japan. However, he could meet neither the emperor nor Shogun Teruyoshi Ashikaga who reigned in Japan in the name of the emperor. Xavier returned to Yamaguchi again, went to Bungo province in Kyushu and met Daimyo Otomo Sorin. He stayed in Japan for two years and returned to Goa in 1551 as he was concerned about Christianity in India. After that Xavier went to China, fell ill at Shangchuan Island, and passed away.

Xavier was buried in the form of a mummy at the Basilica of Bom Jesus in Goa, a UNESCO World Heritage Site. His remains are still enshrined in this church and are put on display for public viewing in a glass case once in ten years. When the author happened to visit Goa in 2014, he came to know by chance about the public viewing ceremony of the mummy of the saint and could witness in person the remains in a beautifully ornamented glass case.

In 1554, during the same ceremony of veneration, a legend says that a woman had bitten off two small toes from the right foot. They were returned later. In order to convince visitors about this anecdote, the toes of the right foot of the saint's body were displayed. The author also witnessed the two toes missing. Further, in 1614, by the order of the Society of Jesus, Xavier's right arm was severed and is presently preserved in Macao. Subsequently, it is said that his ears and hair were sent to Lisbon in Portugal, teeth to Porto in Portugal, and a part of the breastbone to Tokyo.

Secularism is India's national policy

In 1947, at the time of the partition of India, there were violent confrontations between Hindus and Muslims. Many Muslims did not want to be a part of unified India that had Hindu majority and Muhammad Ali Jinnah, one of the leaders of the independence movement, created Pakistan as a separate country. A large number of Muslims who lived in present-day Indian territory migrated to Pakistan and many Hindus who lived in present-day Pakistan moved to India. During Partition, believers of both the religions attacked one another and many of them were killed.

With this historical background, after gaining Independence, India set 'secularism' as the national policy. On the other hand, Pakistan set Islam as the state religion.

Secularism is the principle wherein politics maintains neutrality from religion and religion also does not interfere in politics.

When the BJP, supported by various Hindu supremacist groups came to power in 1998, confrontations between Hindu nationalists and Muslims got intensified. Memories of half of North India having been dominated by Islam in the medieval age and conflicts at the time of the Partition revived soon.

The Ram Temple in Ayodhya in North India that is believed to have enshrined Lord Ram had been destroyed when Islam dominated India and a mosque had been constructed in its place. Extremist Hindu factions, encouraged by the BJP coming to power, demolished the mosque and revived the Hindu temple. This incident ignited clashes again between Hindus and Muslims in India.

On the other hand, extremist groups such as the Taliban and the ISI emerged in the Islamic world. Cross-border terrorists infiltrate into India quite frequently from Pakistan or Pakistan-controlled Kashmir. India is one of the targets of Islamic extremists.

Prime Minister Narendra Modi of the BJP is a devout Hindu. Some critics brand him as Hindu supremacist. He was alleged to have supported or instigated riots between Hindus and Muslims in Gujarat when he was the chief minister of that state. Before he became the prime minister, in some of the western countries such as America, he was even treated as persona non grata (a diplomatic term meaning 'person not appreciated').

Even today in India if there are some Hindu supremacists, on the one hand, there are Muslims who are taking to extremism, on the other. It is for this very reason that the Indian government is persisting with the principle of secularism in order to maintain the social stability of India.

Fight against caste-based discrimination

Unconstitutional and illegal, and yet persistent
India has been progressing domestically. Its global profile is also on the rise but the practice of caste-based discrimination is the biggest challenge it faces at home. The Constitution, promulgated after Independence, declared the caste system as unconstitutional and illegal but it is still widely prevalent. The practice of caste discrimination is more prevalent in rural areas and government intervention to address such practices is of little effect.

Clockwise from top left: Mahabodhi Temple, Bodh Gaya; Vishwanath Temple, Khajuraho; Basilica of Bom Jesus, Goa; Taj Mahal, Agra. Photos courtesy of the author.

In order to address such social discrimination, the government has adopted many schemes to ameliorate the social conditions of the lower castes. Though such privileges have yielded some results, these are still inadequate. Apparently, Indians can guess the caste and class from a person's facial features and surname to some extent, but it is difficult for foreigners to do so. Without proper understanding in this regard it can be hard for foreigners to interact with Indians.

What is the caste system?

Caste-based discrimination is said to have emerged in the process when the Aryans who entered the Indian subcontinent from the north-west gradually conquered the local Dravidians. Caste owes its origin to the Portuguese term 'casta' (pedigree). In India, it is called varna. There are four varnas and then there are the outcastes who fall outside the varnas.

As is evident from its name, the caste system is a system wherein Aryans distinguished themselves from the locals and placed themselves above them. It is discrimination largely based on occupation, skin colour, and pedigree. It got established as a system over time. Varnas got minutely subdivided depending on the occupation of the person. Occupation-based community is called jati or sub-caste. The number of jatis is said to run into several hundreds or even thousands but strictly speaking, they are countless.

To make things worse, the caste system is closely linked with religion. The primitive religion introduced by the Aryans became Brahmanism following philosophical development and refinement. After Brahmanism lost its substance, Buddhism and Jainism were founded as reformative religions. The main motive behind these religions was that Brahmanism had become defunct, especially when there was a backlash against caste-based discrimination. Buddhism and Buddhist philosophy were subsequently propagated across India and overseas by Emperor Ashoka. Many from the ruling and the trading communities adopted Buddhism. On the other hand, Brahminism transformed to Hinduism by adopting the popular faith.

Hinduism is closely associated with the caste system. It survived as it was highly convenient for the ruling and the upper classes.

Islam that was founded in the Arabian Peninsula in the seventh century spread to the East and West and was also introduced in India. However, Hindus and Hinduism survived this onslaught and so did the caste system.

The four varnas are as follows:

Brahmins are on top of this social hierarchy. They are mostly the priests. They protect the Hindu religion and are responsible for religious ceremonies. They interpret the scriptures and perform the role of explaining Hinduism to the lower classes. Since they perform the sacred role of safeguarding the religion, killing a Brahmin is strictly prohibited. In recent times, Brahmins are not necessarily priests; they are active in various fields such as politics, bureaucracy, entrepreneurship, academics etc.

Next in the social hierarchy are the Kshatriyas. They are the royalty, nobility, servicemen etc. In the present-day context, they are politicians, bureaucrats, army men etc. Their field of activity has also widened.

Third are the Vaishyas. They are also called the commoner class. Traders and upper-class farmers fall in this category. Today Vaishyas are also active as politicians and bureaucrats.

The fourth are the Shudras. Earlier they were the subordinate people such as tenant farmers, medium and small traders, retainers etc. There are quite a few in this category these days who are active as politicians.

Below these four varnas are the Dalits. Earlier they were called untouchables or outcastes (literally, outside the castes). Mahatma Gandhi gave them the respectable name of Harijan (child of Hari/Vishnu). Dalits are also active in politics.

One of the salient features of Hinduism is that a child born to Hindu parents becomes Hindu automatically. Moreover, it is possible for a Hindu to convert to another religion, but it is not possible for people from other religions to convert to Hinduism. This is the difference between Hinduism and other religions.

Hinduism and caste are inseparable and caste pursues Hindus all their life. Many Indians may be reluctant to admit it, and yet the thought 'what is my caste' and 'what is other person's caste' willy-nilly does pervade their thought process.

And it does not end with one's lifetime. One cannot escape from karma (retributive justice) or reincarnation. Buddhism also has the concept of karma or reincarnation but it does not have caste-based discrimination.

The new occupations of recent times do not embrace such notions and clearly do not fit into the jatis of yesteryears. The most typical are IT engineers. Indian IT engineers, after passing out from elite universities such as the Indian Institute of Technology (IIT) are employed both in India and overseas and command high salaries. In their case, there is no caste-based discrimination on the surface. It is mostly merit-based. People from lower and upper castes study together. Though they may be conscious about their caste category, there is little or no discrimination.

Caste may be deep-rooted in the social setting but occupations/professions are no longer clearly determined based on caste.

Caste politics

In the last few decades, caste practices have come to influence party politics quite strongly. Those from lower castes form a political party to safeguard their interests and aspire for political power. It is popularly called caste politics or assertive politics to demand their legitimate rights perceived to have been denied for a long time.

A typical example of it is the BSP which has shown its prowess in the state of UP that has the maximum number of seats (eighty for the Lower House), being the most populous state in the country. It is a political party centred around the lowest castes of Hinduism namely Scheduled Castes (SC), Scheduled Tribes (ST), and Other Backward Classes (OBC). The Dalits also form a part of this political grouping.

And then there are also people from the minority religions such as Sikhism, Islam, Buddhism, and Christianity. They also participate in the political process as they are frustrated with the national parties such as the Congress, and the BJP. While the BJP is perceived and thus criticized for being Hindu supremacist, the Congress is viewed as upper class centric. The BSP is, therefore, defining itself to be just the opposite in this political spectrum.

UP has another regional party. It is the Samajwadi Party. SP is also centred on lower castes. The former party head was Mulayam Singh Yadav and the present party head is his son, Akhilesh Yadav.

The caste system is entrenched in the political system of India. Though elimination of caste-based discrimination is the prime goal of the Constitution, it is a truism that both caste and religion are key determinants in the current politics of the country.

In the state elections held in spring 2017, the BJP had a

sweeping victory bagging three-fourths of the seats (345 out of 502) and both the BSP and SP performed miserably. Though the SP opted for an alliance with the Congress, it fell behind by a great margin. As the largest state and largest population, UP is an important state from the perspective of national politics. In the author's view, the BJP's victory in UP exposed the limitations of caste politics in Indian politics.

Both Atal Bihari Vajpayee, who was the prime minister when the author was posted in India, and Narendra Modi are from the BJP. Both had their constituencies in UP. Similarly, constituencies of the first prime minister, Jawaharlal Nehru, former Congress president, Sonia Gandhi (widow of Rajiv Gandhi who was assassinated) and her son, Rahul Gandhi, are also in UP (Rahul stood for the 2019 general elections from two constituencies).

Tragedies over caste
Tragedies over caste-based discrimination in present-day India are a daily affair.

Foremost are the tragedies over marriage. According to caste practices, in principle, marriage must take place within the same caste. A Brahmin boy must marry a Brahmin girl and a Dalit man a Dalit girl. In principle, since India has the practice of arranged marriage, parents as well as matchmakers arrange marriages between boys and girls from the same caste.

In inter-caste marriage due to love, if the boy is from the upper caste, it is still regarded as a forward marriage but if a girl from the upper caste marries a boy from the lower caste, it is regarded as regressive. The former couple is treated indifferently and is barely accepted socially but the latter case is totally unacceptable. The latter is quite likely to be boycotted by the society. At times, both or one of them may be killed by the parents or the relatives. Such cases are called 'honour killings', meaning thereby that the honour of the family and society is protected by eliminating such 'deviant' couples. Such tragic incidents have been reported from time to time in newspapers but it is only the tip of the iceberg. And in the conservative rural areas, the majority of these incidents occur as caste prejudice is strong.

The Sunday edition of newspapers in India is quite voluminous. It contains matrimonial columns running into several pages. Matrimonial pages are classified according to caste such as Brahmins, Kshatriyas etc. But there is no separate category for the lower castes. And the Shudras and the Dalits do not find space in these columns.

If you see the columns for Brahmins, fair girls seem to be preferred. People themselves write that the girl is beautiful. High academic qualification, MNC job, high salary etc., are regarded as merits. Men advertise tall height, high academic qualification, high salary job etc. Reading such columns can be quite interesting.

However, the real upper class or the rich do not use such newspaper matrimonial columns. They have their own circle or group and they arrange the marriages of their children. In extreme cases, they arrange the marriage of their children as soon as they are born.

Caste-based discrimination is especially strong in villages. Dalits live together on the outskirts of the villages that are not yet modernized and where Dalits are still considered untouchables. They are not supposed to interact with the upper castes. Even the well they draw water from is also separate. There is discrimination even in the farmlands.

The author recommends reading a book titled *The Bandit Queen of India* to know more about the caste problem. It is the autobiography of Phoolan Devi who was a Dalit woman. After having spent half of her life under extreme oppression, she married a dacoit and took revenge against the upper castes. She became a Member of Parliament when the author was posted in India. However, she was later assassinated.

In recent years, televisions and personal computers have made their appearances in villages and individuals even own smartphones. The oppressed lower castes also get an opportunity to know about the current situation in the world. They now borrow money from the landlords, take up tenancy of land, buy seeds and end up paying the major part of their harvest in kind. Earlier the price of the harvest was fixed at the behest of the landlord. Today, as the market price is known to them through the internet, the tiller is at an advantage vis-à-vis the lender.

Reservation system for the lower castes

The Constitution of India prohibits untouchability. Through subsequent revisions of the Constitution, today reservation in jobs in government institutions/organizations, parliament/legislative assemblies, government colleges, and institutes of higher education have been granted to SCs, STs, and OBCs. It is called the reservation system. It is a social welfare public system aimed at raising the standard, both social and economic, of the lower castes.

Reservation is fixed by the central government depending on the ratio of lower caste population to the total population and the state governments do so depending on their population in the total population of the state. For instance, of the total number of seats in the Lok Sabha for which elections are held, 84 seats are reserved for SCs and 47 for STs. Reservation for OBCs is also decided depending on their share of population.

In central government funded higher education institutions, 15 per cent seats are reserved for SCs, 7.5 per cent for STs, and 27 per cent for OBCs.

This at least ensures 'equal opportunity'. However, the system has problems too. There are the castes/communities that are not so low who apply pressure on the government to grant them quotas so as to receive the benefits of the reservation system. On the other hand, upper castes, especially from low economic groups, criticize it by saying that the 'reservation system grants privileges without any merit and hence it is reverse discrimination'.

◆

EXPERIENCES FROM MY DAYS AS A DIPLOMAT (2)

PRO-JAPAN PRESIDENT OF DALIT ORIGIN

K. R. Narayanan was the president of India when the author was posted as the ambassador of Japan to India. President Narayanan was a Dalit. He was a person of noble character and was friendly and commanded respect from the citizens.

On 10 April 1998, the author presented his Letter of Credence to President Narayanan entrusted to him by Emperor Heisei in a ceremony held at the Rashtrapati Bhavan. The Letter of Credence is a formal diplomatic document that is presented by the head of one state to that of another state. The head of the country that dispatches the ambassador entrusts him with a signed document addressed to the head of the counterpart country stating: 'I wish to appoint Hirabayashi as my ambassador extraordinary and plenipotentiary in whom I have complete faith. Kindly accept him as an ambassador from Japan to serve for our two countries.'

The head of the state sending the ambassador literally entrusts the ambassador with full powers. Thus, he is officially Ambassador Extraordinary and Plenipotentiary. The ambassador, only after having presented his credentials to the head of the state of the recipient country, is treated as the ambassador extraordinary and plenipotentiary.

President Narayanan was born in the state of Kerala in South India and worked his way through college. After having worked as a teacher and a journalist, he joined the Ministry of External Affairs and became a diplomat. He was extremely talented and a capable diplomat. This is testified by the choice of his candidature by the Indian government to be appointed as the ambassador to two major countries—China and America.

During his young age, he was posted in Japan, and he and his wife, Usha, were blessed with a daughter in Japan. His wife, Usha, was a Myanmarese (Burmese). It is universally recognized that the couple was highly pro-Japan. Their daughter also later went on to serve as an ambassador of India.

Let me briefly explain how the ceremony of credentials presentation is held.

Many people in Japan must have seen on television a newly posted foreign ambassador going past the Double Bridge leading to the main gate of the Imperial Palace in a chariot sent by the Imperial Household Agency. At the Palace, he/she is given audience to the emperor and presents his/her credentials given by his/her head of the state. The Emperor, after receiving the credentials in the form of Letter of Credence, passes it on to the minister attending the ceremony (usually it is the foreign minister but some other minister attending is not uncommon). Here the ceremony ends.

The author's ceremony for presentation of credentials in New Delhi started with the car sent by the Indian government to pick him up from the embassy on 10 April 1998. The official in charge of the ceremony from the Ministry of External Affairs came to pick up the author, his wife, and an embassy official. At the gate of the Rashtrapati Bhavan (former residence of the British Viceroy in India), only the author got down and boarded the chariot waiting for him at the main gate of the Rashtrapati Bhavan. A military officer from the president's office in a gorgeous dress and the secretary-East in the formal dress of the Ministry of External Affairs also boarded the chariot.

Three scenes from the ceremony of the presentation of credentials. Photos provided to the author by the authorities at the Rashtrapati Bhavan.

The author's wife and the embassy official proceeded in the car to the inner gate through the courtyard and joined other embassy staff invited to the ceremony.

After crossing a large courtyard, the author got down from the chariot at the west entrance and was guided to the dais in the inner courtyard. His wife and the embassy officials were waiting at one corner of the courtyard. About 200 guards of honour from the Indian armed forces, namely, the navy, air force, and army in decorated outfits were lined up in front of the author.

The author stood on the dais while the national anthems of both the nations were played (the first picture). Next, he got down from the dais and paraded in front of the guards of honour (the middle picture) who stood in three rows. The temperature was perhaps in excess of 40 degrees Celsius. The author had chosen a traditional Japanese formal dress, haori and hakama outfit, to express his pride as a Japanese ambassador as well as to impress President Narayanan. Under the scorching sun, he was sweating heavily and yet kept Samurai-style discipline.

Finally, the outdoor ceremony came to an end. The author and his entourage entered the Rashtrapati Bhavan climbing a long flight of stairs. He came into the gorgeous hall named after Emperor Ashoka. There was pin-drop silence in the hall. Senior officials of the President's Office and the Ministry of Foreign Affairs, the author's wife, and embassy officials lined up there.

As the author stood in the centre of the hall a little tense, President Narayanan, accompanied by his wife, entered, led by the military officer in waiting. The author stood upright and with heightened emotions he handed over the Letter of Credence to the president (the third picture). The president glanced through the letter and then handed it to the military officer. With this the ceremony to present the credentials was over. Hereafter, the president and his wife, Madam Usha, were more informal and invited the author, his wife, and the embassy officials over to a nearby hall. There were lively conversations including India's first couple's fond memories of Japan. After a pleasant and courteous interaction, we bid farewell to the president and his wife.

Thereafter, the author was invited by the president many times to various events and functions which were hosted by him. The author has the impression that the president was particularly nice to him. The author also invited the president and the first lady to his residence for a tempura party. Mrs Usha Narayanan often attended ikebana sessions and receptions organized by the author's wife.

◆

1.4 A TROUBLESOME NEIGHBOUR—PAKISTAN

Partition and Independence of India and Pakistan

When British rule in India ended in 1947, India did not become independent as one nation.

After the end of World War II, the power of Great Britain was on the decline. Its national power had diminished due to its surrender to the Japanese army in Southeast Asia and prolonged battle with Germany on the European front. With America joining the war, it won the war against the Axis Powers, but actually 'the empire on which the sun never sets' had the possibility of the 'nation itself setting like the sun'.

After the end of World War II, India's Independence movement gained momentum and pace. Great Britain tried to suppress the Indian National Army (INA), which was helped by Japan, but had to give up on the idea due to resistance from the Indian people. India won independence in August 1947. It was the outcome of the long fight put up by freedom fighters such as Mahatma Gandhi, Jawaharlal Nehru, Muhammad Ali Jinnah, and the INA.

However, there was a bitter confrontation between the majority Hindus and minority Muslims during the freedom movement. When Independence became a reality, Muslims under the leadership of Jinnah talked of a 'two-nation theory' and wanted a separate nation for the Muslims. It was based on the thinking that in a Hindu-majority India, there would be no place for Muslims. Gandhi and the mainstream leaders in the Indian National Congress hoped for a unified India. However, confrontation between both sides escalated into armed conflict and Great Britain had to decide on partition and independence. Ultimately, Great Britain and the freedom movement leaders worked out a formula for independence with the partition of India. A major part of the Indian subcontinent belonged to India, and the western and eastern Muslim-dominated parts (separated by India in between) belonged to Pakistan. Pakistan was divided into East and West. The main part was West Pakistan and eastern part became East Pakistan.

Punjab in the western region was divided into two parts with the eastern part becoming Indian territory and the western part becoming part of West Pakistan. Similarly, as for the Bengal region in the east, the eastern part became Pakistan territory and the western part became the state of West Bengal in India.

Pakistan adopted a form of government with the unity of politics and religion with Islam as the national religion. Pakistan in Urdu means 'land of the pure'. A large number of Muslims in India chose to migrate to Pakistan and almost all the Hindus in Pakistan to India. However, both Hindus and Muslims were persecuted during the process of migration and there was a big turmoil. The partition and independence of both the countries was smeared with blood.

Kashmir: region with uncertain future
India and Pakistan were involved in a series of conflicts over the territorial rights of the Jammu and Kashmir region and have fought many wars so far.

Jammu and Kashmir had a Muslim majority but Maharaja Hari Singh, the Hindu maharaja of the princely state of Jammu and Kashmir, signed the Instrument of Accession to the Union of India. Anticipating this, Pakistan invaded Jammu and Kashmir region in 1947. In the beginning, India wanted the policy of both the countries refraining from intervention to be maintained, but once intervention by Pakistan was confirmed and the maharaja asked for India's help, India attacked Pakistan. It was the first Indo–Pak War. Having the maharaja accede to India through the Instrument of Accession, the United Nations mediated and decided the LOC (Line of Control). This brought the war to an end in 1949.

Mumbai coordinated terror attacks

In 2008, terrorists sent by Pakistan gathered in Mumbai through sea and land routes and carried out a major terror attack. They held people hostage in ten places and attacked eight places, namely, Mumbai's iconic Taj Mahal Palace & Tower, and Oberoi Trident hotels, Victoria Terminus (VT) station (now renamed Chhatrapati Shivaji Terminus) which is also a UNESCO World Heritage Site, Cama and Albless Hospital, the popular Leopold Cafe, Metro Cinema, and Nariman House, a Jewish outreach centre. The Taj Mahal Palace Hotel that was constructed by Jamsetji Nusserwanji Tata, the founder of the Tata Group with a lot of emotions went up in black smoke. The terrorists attacked two other places in other parts of the city. 172 (some put it at 174) people died, of which twenty-six were foreigners and over 300 were injured.

One of the terrorists confessed that they were sent by the Pakistan-based Islamist terrorist group Lashkar-e-Taiba. Nine terrorists were killed in the bloody gunfights between the terrorists and Indian commandos. Only one terrorist, Ajmal Amir Kasab, was captured alive. After a long process of judicial trial, he was found guilty and was sentenced to death. He was hanged subsequently.

In such terror attacks, Pakistan has always denied any involvement. Each time any cross-border terrorist attack happens, India thinks that it is the act of the Pakistan-based terrorist groups, especially the ISI, the Pakistani intelligence agency. However, usually there is no conclusive evidence. According to one theory, the ISI plots and executes terror attacks without consulting the Pakistan government.

It thus transpires that Pakistan is a perpetual source of concern for India. And Pakistan is being fully supported by China, the arch-nemesis of India.

Pakistan has the British style governance system, that is, parliament elected through elections, prime minister chosen by the parliament and bureaucrats nominated by the prime minister. Thus, in form both India and Pakistan are by and large the same and even the president as the head of the state is also the same.

However, Pakistan has the system of unification of state with Islam as the state religion, which is in direct contrast to India where secularism is the national policy as enshrined in the Constitution. Pakistan has experienced coups by the army several times in its history and has been often ruled by the army. Unlike India, it is hard to say that democracy has taken roots in that country. Such discord between India and Pakistan continues even today.

◆

Hiroshi Hirabayashi

EXPERIENCES FROM MY DAYS AS A DIPLOMAT (3)

ON THE BRINK OF THE FOURTH INDO–PAK WAR

When the author was posted in India there was an armed conflict between India and Pakistan and things had escalated almost to the brink of a war.

Catching India off guard, the Pakistani army infiltrated into the Kargil region in Kashmir. It was not a terrorist group as usual but was the regular army of Pakistan that carried out the attack. The Indian army reinforced its forces immediately and counter-attacked and pushed the Pakistani army back into Pakistani territory. There was tension in and outside India and speculation whether it was going to be the outbreak of the fourth Indo–Pak war but things were brought under control with the withdrawal of the Pakistani army. Known as the Kargil War, it left a dirty scar on India–Pakistan relations.

Both India and Pakistan became nuclear powers following India's nuclear experiments in May 1998. Pakistan is no match for India in terms of military force but since the nuclear deterrent is the same, it was quite a bold move on the part of Pakistan to do so. Perhaps the line of thinking in Pakistan was that India will not corner Pakistan at the risk of a nuclear war.

In October 2001, terrorists from Pakistan attacked the Jammu and Kashmir State Legislative Assembly complex in Srinagar. India repulsed the attack but there was no standoff. However, again in 2002, both the countries were on the brink of a war. The cross-border terrorist attack by Pakistani terrorists on Parliament House in December 2001 again escalated tensions between the two countries. Though there was no casualty among the members of parliament, some security personnel were killed. India that had experienced repeated cross-border terrorism with many casualties in Jammu and Kashmir has launched counteroffensives by the security forces but there were never signs of a war.

However, on this occasion, India's patience ran out as it was an attack on the Parliament of India, the temple of democracy of the country. India passed orders for the mobilization of forces and the army began sending troops on a daily basis by rail and road to the Pakistan border. The number was in the range of 500,000. The navy also mobilized marines from Mumbai and warships moved to the Pakistan offshore.

Japanese embassy officials including the author rushed to gather and analyse information on the development. The author carried out frequent exchanges of information with the Indian government and army officials as well as the ambassadors of other countries. Foreign ministers from Japan, America etc., visited both the countries and persuaded them to exercise caution and avoid escalation. During this time, the deployment of soldiers by India to the Pakistan border, Kashmir region, and LOC continued. Seeing this, various countries were concerned that it could escalate into a full-fledged war, since once the soldiers are mobilized in such large numbers it is difficult to withdraw in a short time.

As a result of exchange of information and assessment of the situation, once it was concluded that there was a strong possibility of war, the author decided to evacuate from India. Why was this necessary?

Following nuclear experiments, both countries had announced that they were nuclear powers. If there was war and the Indian army invaded Pakistan, no one could conjecture the consequences when the threshold was crossed. Topographically, it is not difficult for the Indian Army to proceed to the current capital, Islamabad, via the old capital, Lahore. To prevent this and protect the heart of Pakistan, it was possible that the Pakistanis could use tactical nuclear weapons (small atomic bombs) against the Indian Army in its territory. If that happened, India could not have been expected to remain quiet and a nuclear exchange could have been a possibility, it was feared. The author's apprehension was that the 'radioactive fallout' carried by the westerly winds might descend from the skies all the way from Delhi to Kolkata.

One of the important jobs of the Japanese embassy is the protection of Japanese residents and tourists. Along with requesting the Indian government for self-restraint, the author had discussions with his government and prepared for the evacuation of Japanese expatriates. In order to apprise them about the situation and seek understanding of the Japanese expatriates in India, they were assembled in the embassy, were told about the situation in detail and about the possibility of evacuating to a safe city in India or overseas. Japanese expatriates were cooperative in this regard. Even the Foreign Ministry in Japan called over the representatives of the Japanese companies present in India and along with communicating to them about the situation every now and then, they were requested to cooperate in the event of an evacuation.

The procedure for evacuation planned was to urge people to use regular commercial flights and once those flights were suspended, to switch to chartered flights. And despite that if the risk of war became imminent, to be even prepared for using the Self Defence Forces (SDF) transport plane C-130 or the government's exclusive aircraft (two jumbo jets) to airlift the people. Based on instructions from the PMO, SDF headquarters and the transport corps unit of the government's official aircraft at Chitose Airport in Hokkaido began preparations. In fact, the families of Japanese expatriates who were not required to stay in Delhi began leaving Delhi on commercial flights.

Other leading countries, except France and Russia, also did the same. The author had close cooperation with ambassadors of other countries, especially the US. Since the number of American expatriates in India was close to 80,000, it even considered deploying an aircraft carrier to India. Even some of the embassy officials and their family members began leaving the country.

The author even requested the American ambassador to accommodate the Japanese expatriates in the aircraft carrier, if required, and had the informal approval from the US government.

It was exceptional but the Russian and French ambassadors told the author that they would like to wait and watch the situation until the very last minute. The Russian ambassador said that he could bring several aircraft within six hours from Russia to India. Even the French ambassador said that if the need arose, he could ask the troops deployed in the Middle East to do the needful and hence would like to wait and decide on evacuation. Japan did not have a system in place to use the SDF suddenly in case of a crisis.

Japanese as well as other foreign companies began closing down some of their plants in India.

The Japanese government based on a request from the author decided to send chartered flights as the number of commercial flights was becoming inadequate to evacuate people. In fact, one day the chartered flight with the rising sun logo landed in Delhi.

It was quite a dramatic scene and grabbed the attention of Indians.

The Indian government was surprised to see the tension among the leading countries to start the process of evacuation of their residents from India. This was perhaps because it was concerned about the negative impact the situation would have on the Indian economy and international reputation of India. Following careful consideration, the Indian government decided to pull back the troops deployed along the Pakistani border and the naval war ships deployed off the Pakistani coast. The author as well as the Japanese expatriates in India felt relieved. Ultimately, war had been averted. And Japan had had to deploy only one chartered plane.

The evacuation of Japanese expatriates in India was the last resort. The planning and preparation took place in anticipation of criticism such as 'premature evacuation', 'wrong judgement of the situation by the ambassador' or 'waste of money' in the event of no outbreak of war. However, the author also thought that just in case evacuation got delayed, there was the nuclear threat looming large and could lead to an awkward situation. Thus, the author was mentally prepared for criticism for having played safe anticipating the worst possible scenario.

There was an old anecdote at the back of the author's mind.

At the time of Iran–Iraq War that lasted from September 1980 to August 1988, the Japanese government was in a dilemma about the evacuation of Japanese expatriates from Tehran. 215 Japanese residents in Tehran stayed till the last minute. Once the war escalated, it was not possible to evacuate them by means of regular commercial flights and the Japanese government was in a fix. Japan Airlines developed cold feet to send a rescue plane and it was difficult to even send an SDF military plane.

Seeing the dilemma of the Japanese government, the Turkish government sent two planes to Tehran in spite of possible risk and succeeded in evacuating the stranded Japanese from Tehran to Istanbul. On being asked 'Why are you doing this?' PM Özal Turgut of Turkey replied, 'I want to repay the favour done by Japan a hundred years ago.'

What was this favour done a hundred years ago?

In June 1890, a naval vessel named *Ertugrul* of the Ottoman empire of Turkey visited Japan on a goodwill visit and presented an official letter from the Turkish emperor to the Meiji emperor. On its return journey in September, it was wrecked off the coast of Wakayama prefecture to the south of Osaka due to a violent typhoon. People from Wakayama prefecture carried out rescue activities amidst the storm and rescued sixty-nine people although 587 people lost their lives. The then Japanese government sent the survivors and the bodies of those dead back home in two navy warships. Sending the dead bodies of foreigners in a warship is an act of international courtesy denoting the highest level of respect. The Turkish people still remember that incident and it is also mentioned in their school textbooks.

2

THE ORIGINS OF PRO-JAPAN INDIA

2.1 THE INDIAN VIEW OF JAPAN

Stories about Japan by the author of *Slumdog Millionaire*
The movie *Slumdog Millionaire*, that won eight Oscars at the Academy Awards in 2009, was an adaptation of a novel by an Indian author. The original novel was entitled *Q & A* and the author was Vikas Swarup. Mr Swarup, who made his debut as a writer with this work in 2005, is a diplomat in active service. He was the official spokesperson of the Ministry of External Affairs in New Delhi (2015–17) and has also been India's High Commissioner to Canada.

Mr Swarup was the Indian Consul General in Osaka-Kobe from 2009 to 2013. In one of his lectures at that time, he had made some observations which were published by the author in the monthly magazine *Jikei* (self-vigilance) of the Tokyo Metropolitan Police Agency. Later, the author included it in his book in Japanese, *World is Pro-Japan Except Those Countries*. Here the author would like to introduce it yet again. It is an eloquent praise of Japan befitting a literati.

Japan is unique because of its homogeneity and its extraordinary culture. I believe a society is defined by the values which underpin its culture. And Japan has a very cohesive society with strong values and ethics. While Westerners are digital, the Japanese are analogue. While Western people are individuals who have intrinsic merit of their own and who do not feel the need to define themselves in terms of other people, Japanese can only operate as part of a larger system, like one hand on the face of an analogue clock, only of value when in a relationship with somebody or something else.

In my last posting in South Africa before I came to Japan, I slept with eight locks, two grills, and sensor beams and alarms all around the house. Here, quite often, we go out for a stroll with the front door unlocked. I see women riding their bikes in the middle of the night. A five-year-old walks home from school unsupervised and alone. Safety is paramount.

But what really amazes me, though, is that even if you misplace your wallet, you have a very good chance of getting it back. Many of my Japanese friends ask me why I don't write a novel about Japan. I tell them that all my novels involve some kind of transference. Somebody's briefcase full of cash gets in the hands of someone else; somebody's diamond ring falls into the hands of someone else. That is what moves my plot forward. But in Japan, even if I deliberately drop my wallet on the road, someone will pick it up and run after me to return it. So, how will my story move? My wife, Aparna, misplaced her cellphone in the Unzen National Park in western Kyushu. We tried to search for it and did not find it. But two hours later we got a call from the police and a policeman personally came to our hotel to return the cellphone which a Japanese tourist had deposited with the nearest 'koban' (a small police station).

The people I have met here are some of the nicest, most genuine people I have ever met in my life. Their kindness and manners are forever imprinted on our hearts. If you ask a passing stranger if they know where a particular shop is and if they don't immediately know the answer, they'll often start researching the subject on your behalf, whipping out their smartphones to locate it using Google maps or calling up their friends for advice. And, after peering at maps and placing phone calls, they'll personally escort you to the place, even if it happens to be half a kilometer away!

I am told that preserving or maintaining the 'Wa', which means 'harmony', is of the utmost importance in Japan. No one blows car horns in a traffic jam. No one writes graffiti on the walls. No one litters the streets. I think that the respect shown by Japanese, young and old, to the environment they live in and the people around them is a beautiful thing and is partly what makes Japan so great.

One of the first visitors I received on arriving in Osaka was the police inspector of the local ward. Now in most countries if an inspector comes to visit, he will only bring handcuffs. But this Japanese inspector brought me a gift, a delicious pack of grapes. Another thing I'm fascinated with is the Japanese love for tradition and ceremony. And living like a local over an extended period of time has enabled us to experience all the traditional events and activities associated with different times of the year.

If tradition is seamlessly integrated into the daily life of the people, so is religion, just like in India. Even in the busiest street or in the middle of a rural backwater, you will find a temple or a shrine. Kyoto alone has 1600 temples and 400 shrines which are oases of peace and tranquility. And whenever I've stopped by a local temple or shrine, I have found someone pausing for a moment of prayer. It's a bit ironic that in hyper technological Japan with its fast-paced lifestyle, people still find time to feed their souls.

From religion also springs the Japanese sense of beauty. For the Japanese, beauty is 'an inseparable part of life itself.' In Japan they say, Beauty is Truth.

Japan has been blessed with abundant natural beauty. We've also seen plenty of Japan's man-made wonders, from the world's longest suspension bridge in Akashi linking Honshu and Shikoku island to the west of Kobe, to the world's tallest tower (Sky Tree in Tokyo), to one of the world's fastest supercomputers.

The natural beauty of Japan is miniaturized and brought down to human scale. What is amazing about Japanese culture is that it has taken the natural beauty in the world around it to develop and perfect an inner beauty, a distinct sense of aesthetics. Today, scholars use terms like wabi sabi, mono no aware, and ma, to explain how Japanese attitudes towards nature have influenced their art and culture. The sakura or cherry blossom tree is the epitome of this conception of beauty; and ma to an empty or formless beauty, manifest in Japanese living architecture, garden design, music, flower arrangements (Ikebana) and poetry. Even the humble bento box becomes a work of art.

If Tokyo has the highest number of restaurants in the world, Japan also has the most vending machines per capita. This is because technology is embedded in the Japanese lifestyle, from the first bullet trains in the world to cell phones whose screens double up as TVs, to the amazing toilets with heated seat and array of buttons which do everything for you. Almost all modern buildings are completely earthquake resistant. There are multi-story, robot-operated parking garages, touchscreen menus at many bars and restaurants, home vacuum robots, and even square watermelons!

Japanese cities are also some of the most organized in the world. They are the cleanest cities I have ever seen. Public transportation in Japan is out of this world. Public transportation is quick, convenient, practical, and always on time. The amazing postal and parcel service of Japan is another marvel, delivering just about anything to anywhere—all over Japan.

This is a society that still believes in honour and devotion to duty. To these I can add the values of honesty, loyalty, sharing, and sacrifice. The whole world saw the best qualities of Japan during the triple disaster of March 2011. Japanese people stayed calm in the face of disaster, making sure to help each other through the earthquake and tsunami that demolished several towns. Despite the harsh conditions, there was no panic or hysteria. No complaining or fighting. No looting or stealing of the sort seen in other countries after a natural disaster.

No wonder, anyone who comes to Japan, falls in love with it. And everyone goes back with a story of everyday generosity and kindness that is typical of the Japanese. So the rest of the world has much to learn from Japan. Japan shows us how to become modern while maintaining traditional values. Japan shows us how to perform your duty with decency and honour. These enduring values may well be the most valuable way in which Japan can offer leadership to the 21st century world.

These are the images of Japan I will take with me. Nature. Temples. Cherry blossoms. And perfect serenity. In this hectic, crowded world, it is rare to experience perfect serenity. We received this perfect serenity in Japan.

Japan and India are siblings

There may be people who might think the above observations to be diplomatic, and yet it may not be wrong to consider them as a summarization of the Indian view of Japan as a whole. Indian people respect Japanese people, and the Indian government and companies rate Japan very high. Indians believe that both people are like siblings bound by a spiritual bond and basic values such as democracy and freedom. And in the field of economy, India regards Japan as a senior as well as a mentor, and has tried to learn from Japan.

India–Japan relations date back to the period when Buddhism that originated in India reached Japanese shores via China and Korea centuries ago. Bilateral ties, however, developed from the latter half of the Meiji period. Leaders of Japan's political, business, and cultural worlds paid close attention to India's importance and future potential. The period of social upheaval in the pre-war Showa period was also the climaxing of India's freedom struggle and Japan's volunteers supported India's cause of independence.

After the war, Japan was placed under the occupation forces of the Allied powers under the control of General Douglas MacArthur as the supreme commander. India earned its independence on 15 August 1947, three months after the promulgation of the Japanese Constitution. India's first prime minister, Jawaharlal Nehru, declared India's independence from the Red Fort, a huge palace in Old Delhi built by the Mughals.

(Nehru made an extempore speech on the floor of the parliament famous for its title 'Tryst with Destiny' announcing India's freedom at the stroke of the midnight of 14 August, implying that when the world slept, India awoke to light and freedom.)

India's stance post-independence towards Japan has been extremely pro-Japanese.

◆

PUBLIC OPINION POLL ON JAPAN IN INDIA

Q: What is your image of Japan? (Top three replies)
   1. A country with advanced technology
   2. A peace-loving country
   3. A country with economic strength

Q: Which country do you think is an important partner for India?
   America: 42%, Russia: 26%, Japan: 17%, China: 5%, England: 3%, and Others: 7%

Q: What is your view of present Japan–India relationship?
   Excellent: 20%, Good: 60%, Normal: 17%, Not good: 17%, and Unsure: 2%

Q: What is your view about Japanese investment in India?
   Welcome: 74%, Rather welcome: 21%, Not welcome: 1%

Q: Would you like to study Japanese language?
   Yes, very much: 26%, Yes, if there an opportunity: 45%, and No: 30%

Methodology: Interview

Period: 16 February–17 March 2013

Research Agency: Center for Media Studies

Target: Opinion leaders (1,711 respondents) and general public (501 respondents)

Figures represent opinion leaders only.

◆

2.2 THE GREAT PIONEERS WHO LAID THE FOUNDATION OF JAPAN–INDIA RELATIONS

Great seniors of Meiji period introduced western civilization and systems while respecting the traditional culture of Japan under the spirit of 'Japanese spirit and western wisdom' and guided Japan in becoming a modern and great power. As a result, Japan won two great wars, first fighting and winning against the Chinese Qing dynasty in 1894–95, and then fighting Russia in 1905–06 and winning that too.

With the emergence of Japan as a new Asian power, the world started paying close attention to Asia, and with great expectations. At the turn of the century, leaders from China, British India, Thailand, and the Philippines came to Japan. Among them were Sun Yat-sen from China, Rash Behari Bose from British India, José Rizal from the Philippines, and so on. On the other hand, a trend to attach importance to Asia also emerged in Japan. Such Japanese leaders were Tenshin Okakura, Shigenobu Okuma, Eiichi Shibusawa, and so on.

Okakura, Okuma, and Shibusawa—precursors for Japan–India friendship

After graduating from the Faculty of Literature, Tokyo Imperial University, in 1880, Tenshin Okakura deepened his friendship with America's Ernest Francisco Fenollosa as an art critic. Both of them travelled together in Europe and America between 1886 and 1887. On his return to Japan, Okakura set up the Tokyo School of Fine Arts (presently the Faculty of Fine Arts, Tokyo University of Arts and Music). He visited India between 1901 and 1902 and was associated with the poet Rabindranath Tagore and religious thinker Swami Vivekananda in Calcutta.

Tagore was a patriot who wrote and composed India's national anthem. He was also closely associated with the French author Romain Rolland and scientist Albert Einstein, but owing to his association with Okakura, he developed an interest in Japan and visited Japan five times. Tagore was the first Asian to win the Nobel Prize for Literature in 1913.

Major milestones of Japan–India relations: Pre-World War I

1902: Tenshin Okakura visits India. Beginning of his close friendship with Tagore.

1903: Inception of Japan–India Association (Shigenobu Okuma, Eiichi Shibusawa etc.)

1905: End of Russo–Japanese War. Stimulates India's freedom movement.

1915: Rash Behari Bose takes political asylum in Japan.

1916: Rabindranath Tagore visits Japan (thereafter, visits Japan for a total of five times until 1929.)

Swami Vivekananda, a religious thinker, who hailed from Calcutta (present-day Kolkata), was a leading disciple of Ramakrishna Paramahamsa who founded the Ramakrishna Mission in the latter half of the nineteenth century. He also visited Japan on his way to attend the Parliament of the World's Religions in Chicago in 1893.

Taikan Yokoyama and Shunso Hishida, eminent Japanese painters, who belonged to the first batch of the Tokyo University of Arts and Music, developed an interest in India due to the influence of Okakura. Yokoyama held an exhibition at Calcutta. Tagore belonged to a powerful family of zamindars (landlords who were also contractors for collection of taxes) in Calcutta and even today his palatial house survives as a museum. In the Japan exhibits hall in this museum, there are many pictures on display that are a reflection of his close association with Japan. There are also pictures at the Japan–India Association that felicitated him when Tagore visited Japan.

After the initial interest shown in India by artists, the political and business worlds also began showing interest in India. The key people were Shigenobu Okuma and Eiichi Shibusawa.

Okuma established Tokyo Senmon Gakko (presently, Waseda University) in 1882, and he later entered politics and went on to become the prime minister in 1898.

Shibusawa was a stalwart of the business world and he established nearly 500 companies from Meiji to Taisho eras including the Dai-lchi Kokuritsu Bank (the first national bank in Japan). He is called the 'father of Japanese capitalism'.

Establishment of the Japan–India Association
Okuma and Shibusawa along with Viscount Moriyoshi Nagaoka of the branch family of the Hosokawa clan established the Japan–India Association in 1903. Its members included leaders of the economic and academic worlds as well as Indians from the Tata Group. In the inaugural issue (1909) of the Japan–India Association bulletin, Okuma wrote an article entitled 'Economical Anglo-Japanese Alliance' and Shibusawa wrote on 'Import of Indian cotton and the inception of Bombay route'.

In the introduction, Okuma wrote about India's importance as follows:

> Today fortunately Japan is the only country in the Orient that occupies a position of dominance in the world. It must be grateful to the countries of the Orient for the favour it has received in the past as an advanced nation of the Orient. Formerly Japan received great favour in the form of wisdom of civilization from China and India. They gave Japan the benefit both materialistically and spiritually commensurate with the benefit we are receiving from the Western civilization today. Especially the influence of India on religion, philosophy, and literature or in other words the spiritual front on the Japanese people is extremely large so much so that if you said India it meant the 'Heaven' for the Japanese of yesteryears.

On the other hand, articles by Shibusawa recognized the importance of cotton for the Japanese economy. He wrote about important events such as paving the way for the import of Indian cotton at a low price following negotiations with the Tata Group of India. This followed the line of thinking that instead of leaving the import of Indian cotton to Britain's shipping company, Japan needs to develop a route for the import of cotton from Bombay and inception of the Bombay route by persuading Nippon Yusen Kabushiki Kaisha (NYK) of Japan, and so on.

General Assembly of the Japan–India Association in 1915. Photo courtesy of the JIA Archive.

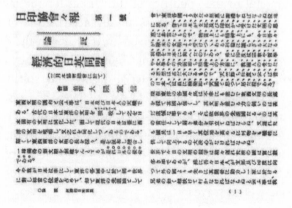

Article by the chairman of JIA, Shigenobu Okuma, that appeared in the first edition of the JIA Bulletin in 1906.

These materials have been preserved by the Japan–India Association.

The Japan–India Association formed in 1903 focused on economic and cultural exchanges with India as Japan still did not have diplomatic ties with British India. The Japan–British Society was established five years later in 1908 for exchanges between the British empire and Japan. The pioneers who focused on India paid more attention to colonial India than the colonial power. The imperial Japanese government needed the Japan–India Association in place of an embassy or consulate. The Japan–India Association established a Japanese products museum in Calcutta.

The Japan–India Association performed the role of carrying out many exchanges with India. It also supported the Indian freedom fighter Rash Behari Bose who had taken asylum in Japan in the pre-war years.

Three founders of the Japan–India Association served as its chairman by turns, Nagaoka as the first, Okuma as the second, and Shibusawa as the third chairman. And the fourth chairman was Nobutsune Okuma (foster son of Shigenobu and President Emeritus of Waseda University). They were all men of prominence.

During World War II, the activities of the Japan–India Association were suspended and resumed after the war. Hisato Ichimada, who later became the governor of the Bank of Japan, became the fifth chairman of the association and Yoshio Sakurauchi, who rose to the position of the speaker of the House of Representatives, served as the sixth chairman. Since 2002, former prime minister, Yoshiro Mori, has been the seventh chairman of the association. The author became the president, a newly created post in 2007, and continues to hold the post till today.

2.3 JAPAN'S CONTRIBUTION TO INDIA'S INDEPENDENCE

India's freedom movement

Since the early seventeenth century, the East India Company that was the vanguard of the British government entered various parts of India and colonized India in due course. Almost inversely with the decline of the Mughal empire, the British dominance of India strengthened and expanded.

However, discontentment against British exploitation of India increased gradually. Revolt against the colonial government in various parts of India began to occur from the latter half of the eighteenth century. There were revolts by the dominant class, ethnic groups at the bottom rung of society, and by Muslims. There were revolts not only in the rural areas but also in the cities.

On the eve of the Meiji Restoration in 1868, there was the 'Sepoy Mutiny' in North India in 1857 which spread to the rest of India within no time. Sepoys were the Indian soldiers recruited by the British East India Company. Towards the end of the Mughal period, the authority of the Mughal empire declined, paving the way for the British to consolidate their domination. The Sepoy Mutiny was especially massive in scale among many anti-British uprisings and the sepoys fought with the support of the Mughals. Since it is regarded as a prelude to a full-scale freedom struggle, it is regarded as a mutiny.

The immediate cause of the mutiny was that the cartridges for the new type of rifle introduced by the British were made from cow and pig fat, the former being a sacred animal of Hindus and the latter considered taboo by Muslims. Here, it was a big blunder on the part of the East India Company that had been involved in India for nearly 250 years to have ignored the religious sentiments of Indians.

The mutiny was led by the upper-class Hindus and Muslims but it spread to landlords, urban people, and farmers. There were even some princely states, partners of the British in the latter's policy of divide and rule of India, that participated in this mutiny. This mutiny was large in scale and was of pan-India scale. The mutiny in Delhi was suppressed by the British army in four months but the fight in other regions continued until 1859.

The British government blamed the East India Company for it and decided to liquidate the company and opted for transference of its functions to the British Crown. The British rulers exiled Bahadur Shah Zafar, the last Mughal emperor, to Burma and in 1858 it passed the Government of India Act. A viceroy was appointed as the representative of the British government and with that the British Raj started in India. Bahadur Shah Zafar died in Burma in 1862.

The British empire was successful in the industrial revolution, and besides exporting cheap Indian cotton in large quantities, it started the exploitation of India when it adopted measures to obstruct the export of cotton products made by Indians. This led to the building of resentment against the British among Indians.

Thus, a movement aimed at becoming independent from British rule gained momentum among leaders of various fields in India. Prominent among them was Mahatma Gandhi. Mahatma means a 'great soul' and the name was given to him by Rabindranath Tagore. Gandhi was born in 1869 in the family of the dewan of the princely state of Porbandar in present-day Gujarat. Gandhi talked about equality all through his life but he himself hailed from a distinguished family.

He studied in England and was a lawyer by profession and was working in South Africa. However, South Africa was a country of apartheid (racial discrimination). While he himself was subjected to humiliation, he fought against discrimination against Indians in that country. He was arrested and sent to jail. Gandhi's resolve to liberate India from the British developed at this time.

Gandhi returned to India in 1915. World War I had broken out a year earlier. Britain enlisted Indian soldiers in exchange for autonomy to India. However, after the end of the war, as England was reluctant to fulfil its promise, the desire of Indians to liberate their country became even stronger and gained momentum.

Gandhi joined the Congress that had been engaged in India's freedom movement till then.

On 13 April 1919, British troops fired at a peaceful congregation in Jallianwala Bagh in Amritsar leaving hundreds dead and many more wounded. This carnage changed the narrative of the freedom movement decisively. The order to shoot was given by Brigadier General Reginald Edward Harry Dyer. This tragic event is etched in the memory of Indians, especially Sikhs, even today as a terrible nightmare.

The Jallianwala Bagh incident led to Gandhi's total commitment to India's freedom movement. However, the novelty of Gandhi's approach was not to resort to violence. He called for 'non-violence' and 'civil disobedience' as methods of protest. Therefore, while being subjected to arrest and suppression by the colonial government, he escalated his struggle into a national movement.

Leaders such as Jawaharlal Nehru and Muhammad Ali Jinnah (the founder of Pakistan) resonated with Gandhi. Among the freedom fighters were Rash Behari Bose and Aiyappan Pillai Madhavan Nair, who took asylum in Japan, and lobbied for support for India's freedom movement.

Following them, Subhas Chandra Bose also came to Japan.

Japanese support for India's freedom movement

Japan searched for a new way out in Southeast Asia owing to the need to recover from the adverse situation in the Pacific war, especially the need to secure resources. At that time, Vietnam, the Malay Peninsula, and Indonesia were under the French, British, and Dutch control respectively. Japan destroyed these suzerain powers one by one after fierce battles. In February 1942, British Lieutenant General Arthur Ernest Percival surrendered to General Tomoyuki Yamashita of the Imperial Japanese Army in Singapore and 'the empire on which the sun never sets' had been defeated.

Prior to this, in 1941, as a preparation for future war with Great Britain, Japan had begun approaching the Indian troops in the British army in the Malay Peninsula. When the battle in the Malay Peninsula got intense and the British army began to lose, Indian troops were distressed. The Japanese army incepted the Indian National Army (INA) in the Malay Peninsula with the help of General Mohan Singh.

In Tokyo, freedom fighters such as Rash Behari Bose and A. M. Nair, who had taken asylum in Japan and had established the Indian Independence League, tried to regain control of the INA from Mohan Singh. Owing to violent behaviour and lower rank in the army, Mohan Singh failed to keep a hold on the INA. On the other hand, Rash Behari Bose had low popularity among the Indian soldiers and was prone to sickness. Therefore, the Japanese army, on the advice of A. M. Nair, decided to invite another Bose, that is, Subhas Chandra Bose, who had taken refuge in Germany.

Subhas Chandra Bose was a part of the independence movement as a heavyweight of the Indian National Congress, but he was of the opinion that taking up arms was unavoidable for the freedom of India and therefore parted ways with the non-violence group, which was the group following Gandhi. In 1924, the British colonial government arrested and imprisoned Subhas Chandra Bose. He was elected the mayor of Calcutta in 1930 when he was released from jail, but the colonial government dismissed him. In 1938, Bose was elected president of the Indian National Congress but he had to resign due to difference of opinion on strategy with Gandhi. Bose founded the group called the Forward Bloc.

World War II broke out in 1939 and when the Soviet Union and Germany and subsequently Germany and Great Britain went to war, Bose thought that the time for India's independence was opportune. Bose escaped from Calcutta to seek help from the Soviet Union for India's freedom. He first reached Germany via Kabul and Moscow and requested Nazi Germany for help. Germany was indifferent to him. Hitler called Bose 'a big braggart of Asia who loiters around Europe' and in his book, *My Struggle*, he wrote that 'it will be better that India is ruled by Britain than any other country'. Besides racial prejudice, Hitler believed that Bose could be a hurdle in the path of reconciliation between Britain and Germany. Bose cooperated with Germany in its anti-British propaganda but could not deny a sense of humiliation.

Amidst such circumstances, Bose received an invitation from Japan, thanks to Rash Behari Bose's lobbying with the Japanese government. Bose left Germany, travelling by German and Japanese submarines, and by plane, and arrived in May 1943. In July, the General Assembly of the Indian Independence League was held and Rash Behari Bose not only gave up his position of head of the League in favour of Subhas Chandra Bose, but made him the commander of the

INA. Subhas Chandra Bose made a speech in front of excited Indian soldiers and announced, 'Dilli chalo'. (Let us march to Delhi.) On 21 October 1943, he proclaimed the establishment of a provisional independent Indian government and declared war against Britain and America.

Subhas Chandra Bose as commander-in-chief of the INA. Photo courtesy of the JIA Archive.

In 1944, Japan planned an invasion of Northeast India to snap the supply route of the Allied powers (Chiang support route) to China. The INA that had expanded to 6,000 soldiers participated in the Battle of Imphal. It was an attempt to destroy the British forces in collaboration with Indian soldiers and liberate India. The Japanese army and INA soldiers entered Northeast India from Burma crossing the Arakan Mountains and advanced to Imphal (present-day capital of Manipur) and further to Kohima (present-day capital of Nagaland). The people of Northeast India resemble Japanese people in physique and features and they were very kind to the Japanese army.

However, the Battle of Imphal was a reckless one carried out under severe weather conditions, without any support of the air force and proper supply of ammunition and food. Ultimately, the Japanese army lost and retreated to Burma, and while withdrawing, it also had many casualties due to lack of food supplies and malaria. The INA lost about 4,500 soldiers.

Around Imphal and Kohima one can still find a strong imprint of the Battle of Imphal. There are tombs and monuments in the memory of soldiers of the Japanese army. The present-day residents are still highly pro-Japanese. The collection of ashes of Japanese soldiers continues even today.

On 15 August 1945, when Japan surrendered, Subhas Chandra Bose planned to check whether he could expect support from the Soviet Union. In any case, he decided to head to Japan but on his way his aircraft supposedly met with an accident resulting in his death.

Japanese officials who were posted in Taiwan cremated him locally and his ashes were brought to Renkoji Temple, Higashi Koenji, in Suginami-Ku, Tokyo. His ashes are enshrined here and on 18 August every year a memorial service is held and Japanese people, who were involved in the Battle of Imphal, their descendants, and enthusiasts of Japan–India friendship, including members of the Japan–India Association, gather here.

However, the reaction of successive governments in India has been vague about Subhas Chandra Bose. In India, many people believe that Bose did not die in Taipei but successfully moved to the Soviet Union. It is similar to the legend of Minamoto no Yoshitsune, hero of the Kamakura period, which makes one believe that he did not die in the Battle of Koromogawa in northern Japan in 1188 but survived and went to Mongolia and resurfaced as Genghis Khan. So far Indian governments have carried out investigations on three occasions of the ashes to find out whether they are authentic, but there was no clear conclusion. In Japan, there are many people who want the ashes to be handed over to India at the earliest, and yet there are no takers. Among the direct descendants of Bose is his daughter, Anita, who is married to a German, and lives in Germany. It is said that only recently she has agreed to a DNA test.

Post-Independence, there were opinions for and against Subhas Chandra Bose within the Indian National Congress, but today he is regarded as a hero. The airport in Kolkata is named after him and there is a portrait of him in the Indian Parliament House. 'Netaji' is the title of Bose which means 'respected leader'.

The author visited Kolkata when he was writing the manuscript of this book in March 2017 and visited both the Tagore House and Subhas Chandra Bose Memorial (Netaji Bhawan, original house of the Bose family) after a long gap. He met two members of the Bose family with whom he had close interactions during his posting in India. One is Krishna Bose, head of the Memorial, and former chairperson of the Lok Sabha Foreign Relations Committee, who is the widow of Sisir Kumar Bose, son of Sarat Chandra Bose, elder brother of Subhas Chandra Bose. The other was her second son, Sugata Bose, former Member of Parliament and professor of history and diplomacy at Harvard University. Besides examining personal items and photographs of Bose yet again, he had emotional discussions with them.

Indecision about bringing back Netaji's ashes to India

leaves a bad aftertaste in the mouth. As a personal opinion, the author discussed with both of them about dividing the remains into two portions and bringing one portion to India and retaining the other portion in the Renkoji Temple. It was because the part brought to India will not be buried but as per the Hindu practice is most likely to be immersed in a holy river (the Ganges flows near Kolkata) or in the sea. The two members of the Bose family, while wondering why recent Indian prime ministers and Indian ambassadors posted in Japan had not visited the Renkoji Temple, expressed their expectation about a quick decision by the Indian government in this regard. They showed interest in dividing the ashes into two parts and also mentioned that if the ashes are to be brought back, they may be scattered but there is also a possibility of the ashes being buried in a special place.

The author sincerely hopes that the soul of this hero of India rests in peace at the earliest.

2.4 PRO-JAPAN STANCE OF INDIA IN POST-WAR YEARS

Indian elephants—the messengers of friendship

During World War II, beasts of prey in Japanese zoos were all poisoned to death. It was a measure to prevent them from escaping out of the zoos and harming the population in the event of air raids by Allied powers on Japanese cities.

One of the new study methods for democracy in post-war Japan was a Children's Parliament. Its aim was to appeal to the outside world based on discussions by children imitating the National Diet or regional assembly. In May 1949, the Children's Parliament of Taito-ku ward, Tokyo, resolved to 'invite an elephant to Ueno Zoo'. Out of curiosity to see rare animals, the children were eager to see an elephant. This resolution was sent to Tsuneo Matsudaira, president, House of Councillors of the Diet, so much so that the Diet decided to take action. Indian traders offered to cooperate and the letter written by children was delivered by them to Prime Minister Jawaharlal Nehru. He was moved by the letter and chose a fifteen-year-old female elephant used for lumber operations in the old capital of Karnataka in South India. Nehru named the elephant Indira after his daughter and sent her to Japan. Indira left India in August 1949 and arrived in Shibaura Port in Tokyo in September and was walked to Ueno Zoo. It was midnight but citizens lined the road.

Prime Minister Jawaharlal Nehru with his daughter, Indira, at Ueno Zoo.

In the presentation ceremony held on 1 October, nearly 50,000 people participated. Prime Minister Shigeru Yoshida, who rarely attended such ceremonies, also came to Ueno Zoo. The representative of the Indian government in Japan read out the letter from Nehru to the Japanese prime minister.

It was a gesture of friendship on the part of Nehru towards Japan to have sent an elephant named after his daughter. The elephant Indira was loved by the Japanese and she died at the age of forty-nine in 1983.

At that time, Indira Gandhi, who had succeeded her father, was the prime minister. In the following year, she sent two female elephants, named by herself as Asha and Daya to Ueno Zoo as her own gesture of friendship. In the Hindi language their names mean 'hope' and 'mercy' respectively. Today, there are three elephants donated subsequently by India to Ueno Zoo.

◆

EXPERIENCES FROM MY DAYS AS A DIPLOMAT (4)

INDIAN DEFENCE MINISTER TOO GIFTS AN ELEPHANT TO JAPAN

During his tenure as the ambassador to India, one of the important dignitaries that the author was close to was Minister of Defence, George Fernandes. One day the author was invited by him to his residence. While chatting about various things, the author mentioned anecdotes about Indira, Asha, and Daya. At that time, the author knew that Fernandes' companion, Jaya Jaitly, is the daughter of Krishna Chettur who participated in the presentation ceremony of the elephant, Indira, to Ueno Zoo. George Fernandes was surprised and told the author that if there is such coincidence, he, too, would like to donate an elephant. The author willingly agreed to the idea and communicated the same to the Japanese Foreign Ministry and Ueno Zoo. Obviously, Ueno Zoo welcomed it.

Mr Fernandes then consulted the author about the name of the elephant. The author replied that the presenter has the privilege to give a name. After a while, he asked, 'How about Surya?' Surya is the name of the sun god in Hinduism. The reason given by the minister was that Japan is the 'Land of the Rising Sun'. The author was deeply impressed that the minister viewed Japan with such an eye. Mr Fernandes selected an elephant from Bihar in North India where his constituency was located. Unfortunately, the elephant died while being transported to Delhi by train. The author thought that the idea would be shelved. But the minister did not give up and found another elephant and it was successfully sent to Ueno Zoo.

Consequently today, there are three elephants, Asha, Daya, and Surya, in Ueno Zoo as goodwill envoys of India who please the visitors coming to the zoo. In front of the shed for the elephants is a bronze plate on which friendly greetings from Jawaharlal Nehru and Indira Gandhi are inscribed, though rusted due to weathering. Thereupon, the author came up with an idea and in March 2008, after discussions with Chairman Mr Mori, the Japan–India Association gifted a big signboard with easy-to-read panels of copper plate with explanatory texts.

◆

India's friendly gestures towards a defeated nation—Japan

The Allied powers led by the US set up the International Military Tribunal for the Far East (IMTFE) to try Japan for war crimes. The sitting commenced from May 1946 and the verdicts were handed down in November 1948.

Seven defendants, including former prime ministers Tojo Hideki and Koki Hirota, were sentenced to death, sixteen persons, including former prime minister Kiichiro Hiranuma, were sentenced to life imprisonment, former foreign minister Shigenori Togo was sentenced to twenty years in prison, and former foreign minister Mamoru Shigemitsu to seven years in prison, and so on.

There were a total of eleven judges in the IMTFE. They were from each of the Allied powers, but the only expert of international law was Radhabinod Pal, a jurist at the Calcutta High Court. Justice Pal wrote a minority opinion against the majority opinions and handed down a 'not-guilty' dissenting judgement for all the defendants.

According to the general rule of criminal law, ex post facto law cannot be retrospectively applied. The rule is that any concept for punishment instituted after a crime or an act has been committed cannot be applied for the concerned crime or act. Justice Radhabinod Pal's claim was that the 'crime against peace' and the 'crime against humanity' as the counts for conviction were concepts introduced after the war. To be more precise, since it is the ex post facto law introduced after the war during which the 'crime' was committed, it cannot be applied for the defendants. Inspired by this, Judge Bernard Victor Aloysius Röling from the Netherlands gave a separate dissenting note and claimed the non-application of 'crime against peace' and opposed the death penalty.

The views of Justice Radhabinod Pal were based primarily on legal arguments.

However, in the author's view, at the bottom of his dissenting opinion there was some appreciation of Japan which, by way of helping two major freedom fighters of India, namely Rash Behari Bose and Subhas Chandra Bose, contributed to the eventual independence of India. It is natural to think that he had repulsion against the western powers and sympathy for Japan. By the way, India won its independence from Great Britain in August 1947 while the IMTFE was still on.

After the war, Japan with scant domestic natural resources needed to import natural resources from overseas. Such resources were critical for reviving the country's economy ravaged by the war. In particular, iron ore was crucial. India had a surplus of iron ore, which it started exporting to Japan. It was believed to be due to commercial reasons, but in the backdrop was the pro-Japanese stance of the Indian government.

India boycotting the San Francisco Peace Treaty and signing a separate Treaty of Peace with Japan

The victorious nations assembled in San Francisco in September 1951 to conclude a peace treaty with Japan. Fifty-two countries participated in it. India, Yugoslavia, and Burma were invited but they did not participate for different reasons. The Soviet Union and two other countries participated but refused to sign it. Forty-nine countries, including Japan, signed the treaty.

Besides the procedural reasons, countries such as China, whose participation was regarded as extremely crucial, did not participate, India's refusal to participate was due to its dissatisfaction with the draft of the treaty having been prepared primarily by the US and Great Britain.

Following several deliberations, India proposed two conditions for participation in the Peace Treaty Conference. But the US did not accept them. The first condition was to give Japan a proper position of honour and equality among the community of free nations and the second condition was that all those countries that had an interest in stability and sustenance of peace in the East must sign the treaty, sooner or later.

In the first condition mentioned above, India underlined that (1) It is difficult to accept placing Japanese Ryukyu and Ogasawara islands, that are historically a part of the Japanese territory and were not acquired based on military aggression, under American control by stationing American troops there; and (2) The US–Japan Security Alliance may be signed after (not before) Japan regains its sovereignty and only if Japan wishes to do so.

And in the second condition, India was of the view that Taiwan should be returned to China and Karafuto (Sakhalin Island) and Chishima (the Kurile Islands) archipelago to the Soviet Union. In the draft treaty, the jurisdiction of Karafuto, Chishima as well as Taiwan was left undefined and remains unclear, a sour point in Japan–Russia relations even today.

When these views of India were rejected, India refused to participate in the Peace Treaty Conference. PM Nehru declared in the Indian Parliament in August 1951 that India would not attend the San Francisco Peace Treaty Conference and would renounce the right to claim compensation from Japan.

Instead, Japan and India concluded a separate bilateral peace treaty in April 1952. Since Japan had regained its independence by then, it matched with Nehru's policy to conclude an equitable peace treaty. In the treaty, both sides agreed to waive all claims against each other. The Japanese Foreign Minister Katsuo Okazaki, who signed the treaty, remarked: 'In this treaty, the spirit of India's friendship towards Japan is quite evident.'

The above response implies that besides India's diplomatic principle of having a 'logical approach' in relations between nations, goodwill towards Japan was quite evident.

Japanese Embassy in India has a prime location
Once diplomatic ties are established, the first and foremost requirement is an embassy. The embassy comprises

the ambassador's office supervised by the ambassador extraordinary and plenipotentiary who is the representative of the sending country and the ambassador's residence where the ambassador resides and hosts diplomatic and social events. It is the face and symbol of the country. Every country wants the embassy to be located in a prime location in the capital of the host country. An especially elegant structure is put up for the ambassador's residence. If one sees the British Embassy (besides the office and the ambassador's residence, accommodation for senior staff is also located inside the embassy premises) along Chidorigafuchi Imperial Moat in Tokyo or the American Embassy in Toranomon area, one can understand not only the practical but symbolic importance of the location. Japanese embassies are also located in prime locations in Washington, D.C., London, Paris, Berlin, and so on, and boast grand elegance.

Post-Independence, the Indian government built a diplomatic enclave in Chanakyapuri in the vicinity of the Rashtrapati Bhavan (the President's House) and invited Japan to construct its embassy there. Even today, embassies of new countries are being constructed in Chanakyapuri. By the way, Chanakya was the name of a statesman who actually lived between 350–283 BCE in India. And 'puri' means a district in a city. Chanakya is also known as Kautilya and was the prime minister and strategist of Chandragupta, the first ruler, of the Maurya dynasty that ruled North India. In other words, he is similar to Zhao Yun Zilong who served Liu Bei Xuande of the Shu Han kingdom in the Chinese classic *Romance of the Three Kingdoms*. In India, Chanakya is usually compared with Machiavelli (known for *The Prince*) of the Italian Renaissance period.

It was perhaps at the discretion of PM Nehru that Japan

was allocated the prime location in the diplomatic enclave. The area houses the ambassador's office, residence etc. This is the largest land size among all the Japanese diplomatic establishments overseas.

In Chanakyapuri, the embassies of major countries are located on both sides of an avenue that is wider than the Champs-Élysées in Paris. On the eastern side, from north to south, are located the embassies of Britain, Australia, Pakistan, Japan, and Germany and on the western side are located the embassies of China, the US, France, Russia, Afghanistan, and Canada.

Incidentally, the Indian embassy in Tokyo faces Chidorigafuchi Moat of the Imperial Palace in the upper Kudan area and is close to the place famous for cherry blossoms overlooking the North Park of the Imperial Palace. And the Indian ambassador's residence is an old mansion of the old feudal lord, Nambu, in West Waseda area.

◆

EXPERIENCES FROM MY DAYS AS A DIPLOMAT (5)

INDIA MOURNED THE DEMISE OF EMPEROR SHOWA

Emperor Showa passed away on 7 January 1989. 'Rites of Imperial Funeral' were held on 24 February at the Shinjuku Gyoen National Garden presided over by Prime Minister Noboru Takeshita. The author was then Director, Management and Coordination Division, Ministry of Foreign Affairs, and was responsible for looking after the guests of honour from overseas. Under the leadership of Foreign Secretary Ryohei Murata (who later served as the Japanese ambassador to the United States and Germany), I was engaged in planning and making arrangements round the clock. Subsequently, the author went to Washington, D.C. to join Ambassador Murata as Minister of Economic Affairs in the Japanese Embassy in the US.

On the day of the 'Rites of Imperial Funeral' it snowed abundantly in Tokyo, as if the heavens were mourning the demise of Emperor Showa and sharing the grief of Japanese nationals. Heads of states such as kings and presidents, crown princes and other royalty, prime ministers, foreign ministers and other ministers from 164 countries as well as other top officials from twenty-seven international organizations, including the United Nations, came to Japan. It was a big mark of respect for Emperor Showa.

Amidst the cold, the entire Cabinet and the Imperial Household Agency were at the service of foreign dignitaries. Even heaters were installed in the tents where they sat.

Respecting protocol, we had a hard time in fixing the seating order. Envoys by rank could be divided into heads of states (kings and presidents), heads of governments (prime ministers), foreign ministers and other ministers, other bureaucrats and ambassadors posted in Japan. Based on international protocol, among heads of states, kings were to get precedence over presidents and for the envoys of the same rank, date of accession or assumption of office was to get precedence. There is no big or small country. For example, Crown Prince Charles of the UK was representing Britain but since he was not the head of state, he was seated after the heads of states but before the prime ministers.

The most difficult task was fixing the sitting order for American President George Walker Bush. Among the heads of states, it was natural to first seat King Baudouin I of Belgium as he was the longest serving monarch; King Hussein bin Talal of Jordan and others were seated based on their year of accession to the throne. Among presidents, French President François Mitterrand, German President Richard Karl Freiherr von Weizsacker and Indian President Ramaswamy Venkataraman also attended the funeral. French President Mitterrand had served longer than President Bush. However, American presidents have a special status for Japan as Japan and the US are bound by the Alliance. Thus, a seating arrangement to put President Bush before President Mitterrand was justified.

The ceremony ended safely without any hiccups. Thereafter, the new Emperor Heisei, son of Emperor Showa, and the Empress Michiko, received each of the envoys in the audience. The audience was on a minute-to-minute or rather second-to-second schedule as the number of guests was so big. Not only the envoys sent by home governments but ambassadors of each country staying in Tokyo were moved by Japan's refined ceremony and unmatched accuracy of time management.

Here, the author would like to mention specially the fact that India, like Japan, declared national mourning on the demise of Emperor Showa. The Indian government announced three days of national mourning from 7 to 9 January 1989.

Neighbouring countries like Nepal, Bhutan, and Sri Lanka also declared national mourning ranging from one to three days. It is an international practice to express condolences on the demise of the head of another state. However, it is very rare to declare national mourning. It signifies the respect Emperor Showa commanded and also that these countries are highly pro-Japan.

◆

The Indian Parliament offers silent prayer every year on the day Hiroshima was bombed

There is yet another thing that denotes India's feelings towards Japan that most Japanese do not know. India attaches great importance to peace and offers silent prayer in the Parliament every year on 6 August in memory of the victims of atomic bombs dropped at Hiroshima and Nagasaki. In this respect, if one excludes the victim nation, Japan, it perhaps has no parallel.

In Japan, there is still a tendency to criticize India for not having signed the Treaty on the Non-Proliferation of Nuclear Weapons (NPT) or for the nuclear experiments in 1998. But these people in Japan often forget to criticize the five other nuclear powers namely, the US, Russia, China, the UK, and France. This is especially true of China, whose nuclear missiles are directed towards Japan, and yet these critics feign indifference to it.

After the nuclear tests in 1998, India declared a voluntary moratorium on further testing to the international society. India has not exported nuclear technology or facilities till date to any foreign country. Though not a member of the NPT, it respects the NPT in spirit. India's nuclear weapon development is the result of the need to have the nuclear deterrent, partly because the five nuclear powers are not fulfilling their obligations for nuclear disarmament as obligated by the NPT and partly because China emerges as a threat to India due to its enhancement of the mass of nuclear warheads.

Indians are of the view that ultimately nuclear arsenals should be eliminated. India is critical of the fact that the NPT is an unequal treaty that recognizes only five nations as nuclear powers. In addition, the five nuclear powers are passive towards nuclear disarmament. In exchange for the promise not to acquire nuclear weapons by non-nuclear weapon states, NPT nuclear states promise to share the benefits of peaceful nuclear technology and to reduce nuclear weapons. India rejects the NPT as a discriminatory treaty against other countries.

◆

EXPERIENCES FROM MY DAYS AS A DIPLOMAT(6)

IN THE MIDST OF INDIA'S NUCLEAR TESTS

In May 1998, two months after the author's assumption of office in India, India conducted nuclear tests. This was the first time it had done so since the previous nuclear tests in 1974. At that time, the then Congress government had carried out the tests to counter China's infiltration into Indian territory in 1972. India that had insisted on total abolishment of nuclear weapons possessed nuclear bombs but had refrained from conducting nuclear tests for long.

In the general elections in spring 1998, the BJP won and was catapulted to power by advocating Hindu supremacy and nationalism. From its election manifesto one got a feeling that it would conduct nuclear tests if voted to power. However, majority of Indians as well as foreign countries did not imagine that India would indeed dare to conduct the nuclear tests that it had refrained from for a quarter of a century. However, on the morning of 11 May, the news of nuclear tests by India came as a bolt out of the blue.

Since nuclear tests need preparation time, the new government must have begun preparations for the nuclear tests soon after assuming power. However, the secret never got leaked out because the preparations must have been carried out by only a handful of people. It is estimated that only Prime Minister Atal Bihari Vajpayee, Home Minister Lal Krishna Advani, Principal Secretary to the Prime Minister Brajesh Mishra, top guns in the army, and scientists associated with it knew about it.

By the way, Defence Minister George Fernandes was the cabinet minister that the author was most close to, but he was not from the BJP and was the head of a party called Samata Party and was nominated as the convener for the coalition NDA government. He supported Tibet's freedom struggle, had a spirit of revolt, organized railway strikes in South India, and was a great friend of Japan.

PROTESTS AND SANCTIONS

Three nuclear tests were carried out on 11 May and two on 13 May. The place was the same as in 1974, that is, the Thar desert in Rajasthan near the Pakistan border; the tests were popularly known as Pokhran-II tests.

Japan and western powers, except France, reacted sharply and imposed economic sanctions against India. Japan stopped the ODA (Official Development Assistance) and suspended ongoing projects in protest. Registering its protests, Japan recalled its ambassador, the author, temporarily for consultations. France refrained from clamping economic sanctions, perhaps because it too had conducted nuclear tests in the southern Pacific some years back.

India also bore the brunt of international criticism such as from the United Nations Security Council, G8 countries, and the International Atomic Energy Agency (IAEA).

The moment he received the news about the nuclear tests on the morning of 11 May, without waiting for instructions from the home government, the author rushed to meet Foreign Secretary Krishnan Raghunath to register his protest. Besides requesting the Indian side to refrain from further tests, the author conveyed to him that the Japanese government would most probably stop the ODA to India to register its protest. The author also emphasized Japan's stance on this issue being the only country to have suffered the impact of atomic bombs. The author could give advance warning on the possibility of stoppage of the ODA without instructions from home as he was confident that his feelings would match with Japan's reaction on this issue. It was also because in the past Japan had stopped grant assistance to China when the latter had conducted nuclear tests. At that time, the author was Director General for Economic Cooperation, responsible for the Japanese ODA policy in the Ministry of Foreign Affairs. Japan had not put a stop to yen loans to China then, as they were already committed officially over a period of five years spanning multiple financial years.

As expected by the author, Kenzo Muraoka, chief cabinet secretary, announced on 12 May the withholding of new grant assistance to India. Japanese ODA to India those days was of three types, namely, grant assistance for poverty reduction and health assistance and other basic human needs to the tune of ¥3 billion annually; yen loans granted for large-sized projects such as power and roads to the tune of ¥130 billion annually; and small amount of technical cooperation. The Japanese government had first given a warning by suspending grant assistance. However, aid for projects that were already promised or had already begun was continued. There was also expectation in Japan for India not conducting any more tests.

On receiving official instructions from the government, the author called on Brajesh Mishra and Krishnan Raghunath on 12 May and communicated the decision of his government. Both did not express any anger on the author's protest and responded quite courteously. Both explained that these tests were unavoidable from India's security point of view. Brajesh Mishra, who was highly trusted by Atal Bihari Vajpayee, said that he could understand Japan's feelings as the only nation to have experienced nuclear bombings and expressed that the Indian government wanted to send an envoy to Japan to explain India's position. The author learnt later that it was Brajesh Mishra himself who was to visit Japan as the envoy.

However, on the following day, India conducted further tests. Japanese government felt that its protest had been ignored. Therefore, it decided to suspend even the yen loans. Projects that were already promised were continued but new ones were suspended.

In addition to protests through the author, Foreign Minister Keizo Obuchi summoned Indian Ambassador to Japan, Siddharth Singh, and lodged a strong protest. Along with refusing to receive the special envoy of the Indian government, the Japanese government decided to call back the author temporarily in the name of 'consultations with the home government'.

'Temporary return for consultations with the home government' is one form of protest in diplomatic practice. 'Calling back its envoy' is one step ahead in this regard. It was a calculated measure considering the timing and gravity of the situation.

By the way, in 2017, Japan recalled its envoy to South Korea, Yasumasa Nagamine, temporarily for consultations to protest against Korean violation of the 'Final and Irreversible Japan–Korea a Agreement' in connection with the problem of so-called comfort women.

The author, on his temporary return to Japan, called on Prime Minister Ryutaro Hashimoto, Foreign Minister Obuchi, and Chief Cabinet Secretary Muraoka and along with apprising them about the situation, received instructions on the future course of action, details of which have been omitted here. Hashimoto instructed the author to resume his duty in New Delhi as early as possible since he thought that instead of prolonging the author's stay in Japan, he would be more useful while performing his role as ambassador and hence should return to India.

The author returned to India in less than a week and focused on communicating the stance of the Japanese government and feelings of the Japanese people to key officials of the Indian government and the media. At that time, he emphasized repeatedly that the protest was not intended at damaging the Japan–India friendship but to prevent the possibility of more nuclear tests and also to make the world know about Japan's stance and feelings as the only country to have suffered atomic bombs.

Being a great friend of Japan, George Fernandes was extremely sorry about it but he explained that nuclear tests were unavoidable from the viewpoint of countering the Chinese nuclear threat and that the subsequent missile tests by India were intended to enhance the capability to target nuclear warheads in China.

Thereafter, the author devoted himself to improving the relationship with India while performing his duties as an ambassador. The ODA had been suspended but the author was often invited to the opening ceremonies of various projects where Japan's role was appreciated.

Following criticism and protests from the international society on nuclear tests, the Indian government has practically maintained the policy of non-proliferation and declared a moratorium on further tests. Even today, there is no change in the Indian government's policy.

Thereafter, India's relations with the international society were gradually restored. Post-2000, various countries, including Japan and the US, lifted economic sanctions against India. Not only that, on 8 October 2008, American President George Walker Bush signed the legislation on the Indo–US nuclear deal. It was approved by the US Congress and made into a law, which was given the name of United States–India Nuclear Cooperation Approval and Non-proliferation Enhancement Act. The UK, France, China, and South Korea also signed similar agreements with India. And finally, in November 2016, Japan became the last leading nation to sign the civil nuclear agreement with India after protracted negotiations. It came into force on 21 July 2017.

For the author, who bore the brunt of nuclear tests, it was an experience of a thousand emotions.

SHOCK DURING THE SPEECH BY PRESIDENT CLINTON IN THE INDIAN PARLIAMENT

Post-1998 nuclear tests, both the Japanese and Indian governments looked for opportunities to normalize relations between the two countries. The US, Canada, the European countries, and Australia that had adopted a tough stance towards India, such as imposing economic sanctions, had a similar approach.

The US was quick in its response and reviewed its India policy. In the months after the nuclear tests, US–India 'Strategic Dialogues' began between the Indian External Affairs Minister Jaswant Singh and US Deputy Secretary of State Strobe Talbott. Western nations having no experience of nuclear bombings did not oppose India as strongly as Japan. The US attached importance to India's strategic and geopolitical significance. These talks were held over fourteen times till September 2000, leading to the visit of President Bill Clinton to India.

President Clinton visited India in March 2000. Since he was to deliver a speech at the Indian Parliament, the author also went to the VIP section for diplomats on the first floor of the Parliament House.

By the way, it is the same practice in all the countries, but it is an exceptional honour for a visiting foreign head of government to be asked to address the parliament of the host country. In the case of Japan, prime ministers Yasuhiro Nakasone and Toshiki Kaifu had addressed the Indian Parliament. In recent times, in August 2007, Prime Minister Shinzo Abe delivered a speech at the Indian Parliament.

President Clinton was welcomed at the Indian Parliament and in the hall, K. R. Narayanan, Atal Bihari Vajpayee, and many cabinet ministers were present. As soon as President Clinton, accompanied by his wife, Hillary Rodham Clinton, and other members of his entourage entered the hall in the Lok Sabha, there was thunderous applause. It was a wonderful speech delivered in a friendly and constructive tone.

However, for the author, a bigger shock came after the completion of President Clinton's speech. Not only did the members of parliament give thunderous applause again, but many of them moved forward to shake hands with President Clinton. Among them, some members even jumped over the long tables in front of them and rushed towards the president and his wife.

VISIT TO INDIA BY PRIME MINISTER MORI AND THE LIFTING OF ECONOMIC SANCTIONS

On returning to the embassy, the author had discussions with his colleagues and conveyed to his home government his view that the Japanese prime minister should also visit India.

Keizo Obuchi was the foreign minister at the time of the nuclear tests. Later, he became prime minister succeeding Ryutaro Hashimoto. Obuchi was highly impressed at the decision of the US president to visit India and the enthusiastic welcome accorded to him by the Indian side. Obuchi agreed in principle to visit India. However, the chronic disease that he suffered from worsened and he had a brain stroke on 2 April 2000 and was hospitalized. When he realized that he was unable to discharge his duty as prime minister, he decided to resign from office. Ultimately, Obuchi passed away on 14 May without hosting the Okinawa Summit or visiting India.

Secretary General of the Liberal Democratic Party Yoshiro Mori was nominated as his successor. The author, since his young days as a bureaucrat at the Ministry of Foreign Affairs, had interactions with Mr Mori, then Member of Parliament. Both were also together in the periodically held non-official Experts' Study Group hosted by the famous journalist and critic, Soichiro Tahara.

The author sent official telegrams to the foreign minister and suggested that Mori should visit India. Like Obuchi, even Mori was quite clear that the future of the world would revolve around information technology (IT). Since India's IT prowess was already proven, Mori decided to visit India.

Yoshiro Mori and his delegation toured South Asia, namely, Pakistan, India, Nepal, and Bangladesh in that order. The sequence was decided based on geographical location and holidays. India and Nepal have Sundays off and

Pakistan and Bangladesh have Fridays off. It is against protocol to ask for official meetings with the head of government of the host country on a holiday.

In India, Mori first visited Bangalore (now called Bengaluru), the capital of Karnataka and the centre of the Indian IT industry. All the state government officials welcomed him with open arms and people lined both sides of the road. Journalists accompanying the prime minister were impressed and touched on seeing this. The next day, at the head office of Infosys, a leading IT company, Chairman N. R. Narayana Murthy enthusiastically welcomed Mori and his team.

Thereafter, Prime Minister Mori moved to Delhi, attended a summit meeting with Prime Minister Vajpayee, and had other engagements. It included a lunch hosted by the prime minister, a courtesy call to President K. R. Narayanan, a reception hosted by the president, courtesy call to Mrs Sonia Gandhi, leader of the Opposition party, and a speech at the Federation of Indian Chambers of Commerce and Industry (FICCI).

As an outcome of the summit talks, a Japan–India Global Partnership for the twenty-first century was announced. Along with promoting a bilateral friendly relationship between Japan and India, it talked about contributing to solving various global problems as leading nations of the world.

The author hosted a reception inviting Japanese expatriates in India along with their spouses in a big hotel and all of them greatly welcomed and appreciated it. Japanese expatriates were greatly pained by the stagnation of business and cultural exchange due to the cooling off of Japan–India relations following the nuclear tests. The Japanese prime minister was literally mobbed but he seemed to be happy and freely posed for photographs with the guests. Since the reception continued way beyond the appointed time, the author had to rush to his residence where another reception for the media was scheduled, leaving the prime minister behind in the hotel. He came soon after but he seemed to have a lingering excitement from the warm welcome he had received from the expatriates.

The author also felt that at last Japan–India relations had again got back on track and felt rewarded for his hard work leading to this epoch-making visit.

The next day, Mori and his entourage visited the Taj Mahal, a famous World Heritage Site. The sun on 25 August was reflecting on the white marble of the Taj Mahal and it was very hot. Everyone was sweating profusely and yet was filled with a sense of satisfaction.

With the visit of Yoshiro Mori, the grant aid that had been stopped due to the protest against nuclear tests was restored. However, more importantly, yen loans were not revived as there was still some ill-feeling in Japan towards India.

It was not until the autumn of 2001 that the ban on yen loans was lifted. On 11 September 2001, there were terrorist attacks in New York City on the World Trade Center and the Pentagon. The twin towers of the World Trade Center were totally destroyed. President Bush declared war on terrorism by the international society.

India was one of the first countries to respond to this call. It was because India had suffered for long from cross-border terrorism in the region of Jammu and Kashmir where terrorists from Pakistan cross the Line of Control—the de facto border between the two countries. The international society welcomed India's stance.

The Japanese government finally decided to lift the ban on yen loans as it felt that it was not logical to continue economic sanctions against a country that was a like-minded comrade in the war against terrorism.

DECLARATION OF JAPAN–INDIA STRATEGIC GLOBAL PARTNERSHIP
Soon after the ban on yen loans was lifted, Prime Minister Atal Bihari Vajpayee visited Japan in December 2001. It was the first visit by an Indian prime minister after a gap of nine years. He had a summit meeting with Prime Minister Junichiro Koizumi of Japan and issued a joint statement for the further promotion of 'Global Partnership'.

Vajpayee first arrived in Osaka and attended a luncheon party hosted by the governor of Osaka prefecture and held discussions with Kansai business leaders.

And, in Tokyo, he had a busy schedule—among others, meeting with the prime minister, and attending a dinner hosted by him, a luncheon party hosted by the emperor, courtesy calls by key ministers and opposition leaders and welcome parties hosted by business federations and Japan–India Parliamentary Friendship League.

Both PM Vajpayee and the author had participated in these events leaning on walking sticks meant for injured persons. Looking at us with sticks, Prime Minister Koizumi had joked saying, 'What is this? Did you both get injured together?' PM Vajpayee's degenerative knee arthritis had worsened and he had undergone surgery performed by a surgeon of Indian origin from America just prior to his departure for Japan, while the author had hurt himself on his left heel when visiting Agra Fort, a World Heritage Site in Agra close to the Taj Mahal, when he fell down a marble bathtub (without water) that had been built for the use of Mughal princesses. Thus, with one stick under his arm he participated in the official functions for PM Vajpayee who, on his part, held his own stick; it was as if the author was giving PM Vajpayee good company.

Japan–India relations progressed smoothly thereafter. 2002 marked the fiftieth anniversary of the signing of the Japan–India Peace Treaty. It was just about time for the author to be transferred, but he requested the Ministry of Foreign Affairs that he move only after the ceremonies and events commemorating the anniversary were over. The request was granted. That year in spring and autumn many cultural events were held in both Japan and India. The author moved to Paris as Japan's ambassador to France at the end of October. Four years and eight months in India were quite turbulent, but he felt quite lucky to be a diplomat during such times.

PM Koizumi visited India in April 2005. Both the prime ministers issued a joint statement on 'Japan–India Partnership in a New Asian Era: Strategic Orientation of the Japan–India Global Partnership' and agreed to implement the 'Eight-fold initiative for strengthening Japan–India Global Partnership'.

In December 2005, it was Prime Minister Dr Manmohan Singh who visited Japan. He and his counterpart Shinzo Abe, who had succeeded Junichiro Koizumi, made an announcement to elevate 'Japan–India Global Partnership' to 'Strategic Global Partnership'. There were several agreements signed in this regard. The most epoch-making one was the decision to hold summit talks every year between the two countries alternately in the capital of each country. India was the first country for Japan to have the prime minister's visit to the partner country every year alternately, and for India it was the second after Russia.

As mentioned earlier, this 'Strategic Global Partnership' was further elevated to 'Special Strategic and Global Partnership' when PM Modi visited Japan in September 2014. There is perhaps no such global partnership in the world that has three adjectives prefixed to it.

MAJOR MILESTONES IN JAPAN–INDIA RELATIONSHIP (NUCLEAR TESTS→MENDING OF RELATIONSHIP→TO A NEW DIMENSION)

1998: Nuclear tests by India and Pakistan. Imposition of sanctions by Japan, the US, and other countries on India.

August 2000: Visit to India by PM Mori and announcement of 'Japan–India Global Partnership'.

September 2001: The 9/11 terrorist attacks in the US. Lifting of ban on yen loans to India.

2006: After elevation to 'Strategic Global Partnership', prime ministers of both the countries visit each other every year alternately.

2013: State visit by His and Her Majesties, Emperor and Empress, to India.

2014: Elevation to 'Special Strategic and Global Partnership.'

◆

2.5 GRATITUDE FOR JAPAN'S ECONOMIC COOPERATION

India as the largest recipient of Japanese ODA

India has been grateful to Japan for its economic and technical cooperation over a long period of time and successive governments have expressed their gratitude to the Japanese government for the same. PM Manmohan Singh who was in office for ten years starting 2004, has mentioned on several occasions that India was bailed out with financial support from Japan in the early 1990s when he was the finance minister and also when India was faced with a foreign exchange crisis during the first Gulf War.

India is the largest recipient of Japanese Official Development Assistance (ODA) over time. India was also the first country to receive yen loans from Japan. In 1958, Japan offered construction funds in the form of yen loans (ODA loan) for a port in India, in order to import iron ore needed from India for its rehabilitation and reconstruction after the war. According to the 'ODA White Paper' published every year by the Ministry of Foreign Affairs of Japan, between 1958 and 2015 India received a total of ¥5 trillion 82 billion, the break-up of which is loan assistance to the tune of ¥ 4 trillion 941.5 billion, grant assistance to the tune of ¥92.2 billion and technical cooperation to the tune of ¥48.3 billion.

India is a huge country, and since it has high demand for infrastructure construction such as roads, railways, water supply, electricity, and so on, the amount of money needed for each project is big and it cannot be covered just by grants. Therefore, the need is very high for yen loans and non-ODA bank funding (for instance, financing by the JBIC). The Indian government has been faithfully fulfilling its repayment obligation. There has never been any default in repayment. It does not betray the trust of its lenders. After all, India has the pride of being a great nation.

On the other hand, grant assistance is offered in areas such as poverty eradication, environmental protection, health, hygiene improvement etc. Assistance for technical cooperation is offered for human resources development such as receiving technical trainees from India and sending experts from Japan. Projects are implemented not just in urban areas, but many small projects at the 'grassroots assistance level' which are implemented by NGOs in various parts of the country are also supported every year.

◆

EXPERIENCES FROM MY DAYS AS A DIPLOMAT (7)

JAPAN RESCUES INDIA FROM THE FOREIGN EXCHANGE CRISIS DUE TO THE GULF WAR

India faced a foreign exchange crisis in 1991. It was caused by the Gulf War.

On 2 August 1990, Iraq led by President Saddam Hussein launched an armed incursion into Kuwait over oil resources in the offshore of the Persian Gulf and annexed it on 8 August. The Iraqi army ran amok in Kuwait. The United Nations demanded the immediate withdrawal of Iraqi forces from Kuwait, but Iraq ignored it. On 29 November, the UN passed a resolution and empowered member countries to use 'all necessary means' to force Iraq out of Kuwait. In January 1991, President Bush deployed American forces to Saudi Arabia. Along with defending Saudi Arabia from Iraq, its aim was to prepare for the subsequent offensive. In response to this, coalition forces from thirty-four countries were formed. The coalition forces launched the air bombing of Iraqi forces occupying Kuwait on 17 January 1991 and ground forces invaded Iraq on 23 February. The battle ended in a short time and Kuwait was liberated. The coalition forces entered Iraq and cornered Iraqi troops. The ceasefire was declared without any personal attack on Saddam Hussein. The US was afraid that if Iraq gets weakened, its long-standing rival, Iran, would become a threat. The fact that Saddam survived coalition attacks became the cause for the second Gulf War later.

Here the author would like to be excused for a little digression.

The author was Minister (Economic Affairs) in the Japanese Embassy in the US when the Gulf War happened. How to deal with the Gulf War was the prime responsibility of the political affairs section, and yet in view of the importance of the matter, Ambassador Ryohei Murata mobilized the entire embassy staff. As a result of repeated negotiations with the US government, the Japanese government promised to contribute initially US$2 billion towards the coalition forces and another US$2 billion aid (mainly yen loans) to the neighbouring countries of Kuwait (Jordan, Egypt, and Turkey).

Although commitments to the coalition were varied, almost all the countries promised contributions of personnel including armed forces. The US requested Japan for contributions of personnel for transporting the coalition forces and others, but those days Japan had neither the legal framework nor the political will to do so. Therefore, the US requested a bigger financial contribution and ultimately Japan committed to contribute an additional US$9 billion. Since Finance Minister Ryutaro Hashimoto in his meeting with US Secretary of Treasury Nicholas F. Brady did not clarify whether Japan's contribution would be in Japanese yen or US dollar, soon thereafter, Japan had to pay off another US$500 million to cover the gap due to depreciation of the yen.

Thus, ultimately Japan contributed a total of US$13.5 billion for the coalition forces and economic assistance to the neighbouring countries. Of this, US$10.5 billion was contributed for the coalition forces (US$9.8 billion for the American forces and US$700 million for the forces of the other countries); US$500 million was to pay off the shortfall due to fall in value of the yen in the foreign exchange market. Japan had to temporarily increase taxes to meet such large amounts of financial contribution. The author learnt later that it was about ¥10,000 per household. Japan became the largest contributing country in terms of financial support in the world. There is no doubt that without it coalition forces would not have been able to function.

However, when three months after the end of the war, Kuwaiti government thanked American-led coalition through advertisements in leading dailies in Washington, D.C., Japan stood out by its omission. Despite the big financial contribution, Japan or the Japanese people's contribution was not visible to the eye because Japan did not send any Japanese military or civilian. It is true of the international society as well as Japan that 'contribution in sweat or with blood rather than money' gets better appreciated. This anecdote became a matter of humiliation for Japan.

And a victory parade was carried out in Pennsylvania Avenue in Washington, D.C., in June. As per the original plan, Ambassador Murata was assigned a seat in the general section and not in the special section for the countries that had contributed to the coalition forces. Ambassador Murata realized it early enough and after talking it over with the Department of State could have included himself in the special section for countries that contributed to the coalition forces. According to him, he was thus able to avert additional humiliation for Japan. This became a 'trauma' for the Japanese and later led to the enactment of the International Peace Cooperation Law and to its first ever application when Japan dispatched the SDF (the UN Peace Keeping Force) to Cambodia.

The above details are described in *Memoirs of Ambassador Ryohei Murata* (Minerva Books). They are also mentioned in the author's book titled *Top Leader's Diplomatic Ability: Prime Minister! You, Yourself, Are the Message.*

The first Gulf War also shook India badly. India had to temporarily evacuate a large number of Indian labourers working in the Gulf to protect them from the war. As a result, remittances that were being sent by them fell sharply. Since the war had occurred in the oil producing belt of the Persian Gulf, crude oil prices also rose sharply. India's foreign exchange reserves that were dependent on foreign exchange remittances and import of crude oil declined rapidly.

Unfortunately, during the election campaigning in May 1991, Prime Minister Rajiv Gandhi was assassinated. P. V. Narasimha Rao was his successor. He appointed as his finance minister a noted economist, Dr Manmohan Singh, who had the experience of serving as governor of the Reserve Bank of India (RBI) and chairman of the Planning Commission.

India's foreign exchange reserves had depleted so much so that they could barely finance two to three weeks of imports. Finance Minister Manmohan Singh immediately approached the International Monetary Fund (IMF), but its response was not encouraging. He then decided to visit Japan and requested Finance Minister Ryutaro Hashimoto to bail out India from this precarious situation. Japan's Finance Ministry discussed the matter with the Bank of Japan. The decision arrived at was to provide India with financial help. The IMF also followed suit. As it transpired subsequently, India was able to avert the crisis thanks to Japan's timely help.

Subsequently, Manmohan Singh, who had emerged as a heavyweight in Indian politics, became prime minister in May 2004 and served two terms for the next ten years.

PM Manmohan Singh talks about this episode and the contribution of Japan's ODA to India at every possible opportunity. Japanese ODA is orthodox in nature, as it is offered mainly for poverty eradication, environmental protection, basic education, and so on, but it is not necessarily conservative. In recent years, large amounts of 'visible aid' such as that for the construction of a Japanese-style metro in major cities including Delhi, the 1,483 kilometres long freight corridor between Delhi–Mumbai and the 500-kilometres long shinkansen (bullet train) project between Mumbai–Ahmedabad, and so on, are outcomes of appreciation and high evaluation of Japan by India.

◆

'Indian manufacturing revolution' by Suzuki

The Suzuki Motor Corporation (SMC) headquartered in Hamamatsu in Shizuoka prefecture decided to invest in India in 1982 when the Cold War was still on. It was due to the wise decision and foresight of President and CEO Osamu Suzuki (the current chairman).

At that time, India was still a state-led economy. The state controlled the key industries and the economy was at the mercy of the administration. Economic growth and national income levels were low and owning a car was beyond the reach of most Indians. Those days the common cars were mostly outdated models such as the 'Ambassador' etc.

Prime Minister Indira Gandhi formulated a plan to manufacture a people's car that the majority of Indians could

buy and was looking for a joint venture partner. It was President
Suzuki of Suzuki Motor Corporation who responded to her
call. Based on a joint venture agreement between the Indian
government and SMC, Maruti Udyog Limited was formed in
February 1981. 'Maruti' means the god of wind and the image
was of a car streaking through the city like the wind. 'Udyog'
means industry or factory.

*Prime Minister Indira Gandhi visiting the factory of Maruti Suzuki with
Chairman–General Manager Osamu Suzuki in 1983.*

Suzuki's success and its contribution to Indian society was
highly appreciated and in 1992 Suzuki's equity was enhanced
from 40 per cent to 50 per cent and became at par with that
of the Indian government. And, in 2002, Suzuki's share was
increased to 54 per cent. In May 2007, the Indian government
exited Maruti and sold off its stake completely. The company
became an entirely private company with Suzuki as the main
shareholder. In September 2007, the company name was also
changed to Maruti Suzuki India Limited, which happens to be
its name till date.

During the author's tenure in India, there was a dispute
between Suzuki and the Indian government over the

appointment of a new managing director (MD). As per the agreement between the two partners, they must have the MD rotate between them every five years. But when the Indian government announced a new MD, President Osamu Suzuki said that the new MD was not suitable for the post. Osamu Suzuki asked the Indian government to change its nominee but the Indian government did not agree. The Suzuki side went to the international arbitration court in London, and both sides finally agreed for reconciliation. As a result, the term of the then MD was curtailed to just over two years and his successor was chosen in consultation with the Suzuki Maruti Corporation.

It may be called a victory for the SMC. In India where there is a strong tone of officialdom, the SMC could take on the government head on and persist with its claim because of Osamu Suzuki's courage, his deep understanding of India and the Indian people, and above all the track record of developing into the top automobile company in India. It is a small-sized car-centric company, and yet it enjoyed two-thirds market share in the Indian market at that time and contributed to technology transfer and employment generation through its plants, vendors, and dealer network spanning the entire country.

Suzuki succeeded in India because of the good offices and support of PM Indira Gandhi and PM Rajiv Gandhi. In addition to the untiring efforts of the SMC, such political weight is even felt by its citizens in a country where there is a strong tradition of making much of officials and little of the people.

According to the author, the biggest contribution of Suzuki's success in India is having brought about a kind of industrial and manufacturing revolution in India. Seeing Suzuki's success, the future direction of industries as a whole and the mindsets of the management across companies have undergone perceptible changes.

Subsequently, automobile manufacturers of various countries who understood the future potential of the Indian automobile industry such as Japan's Honda, Toyota, and Nissan–Renault, America's General Motors and South Korea's Hyundai, and so on, accelerated their investment in India. Despite this, even today, Suzuki's market share is 50 per cent, according to the *Economic Times* dated 4 April 2018.

Honda, along with Yamaha and Kawasaki, had already ventured into the two-wheeler market segment in India. While the author was posted here, Honda also forayed into the four-wheeler market segment. The opening ceremony of its plant in Greater Noida was conducted in typical Indian style with two decorated elephants welcoming the guests by lightly touching their heads with their trunks.

Toyota had once failed in India but was determined to resume its activities with redoubled energy. It set up a joint venture with a medium-sized industrial house, Kirloskar, in Bangalore, the capital of Karnataka in 1997. Its opening ceremony was also held when the author was posted in India and Chairman Shoichiro Toyoda (actually honorary president) proclaimed Toyota's eternal commitment to India. The entry of 'World's Toyota' highlighted the potential of the Indian market not only to Indians but also to the world at large.

Nissan Motors along with Renault opened its plant in the suburbs of Chennai, the capital of Tamil Nadu, in 2010. The author attended the opening ceremony along with Yoshiro Mori, Chairman of the Japan–India Association and was surprised by the huge size of the plant. Chairman Carlos Ghosn who solemnized the opening ceremony mentioned that Nissan plans to manufacture 400,000 cars annually, of which half will be sold domestically and another half will be exported, and announced that Nissan plans to make India the export hub for Asia, Middle East, and Africa.

The strategy to make India the manufacturing and export base is the same in case of other companies too. In addition to its Gurgaon (presently Gurugram) plant, Suzuki built its second plant in Manesar to the south of its first plant. And while this manuscript is being written, it has opened its third plant in Gujarat near the Arabian Sea. This plant is under the direct control of the SMC and is called Suzuki Motor Gujarat.

By the way, the construction of the Delhi–Mumbai Industrial Corridor Project (DMIC), a vital project for both the Japanese and Indian governments, is a work-in-progress and some of the freight cars to be operated on this railway will be double-decker. It is because it will be more efficient to transport small cars manufactured at Gurugram and Manesar plants in these double-decker freight cars. It speaks volumes of Suzuki's influence in India.

Major milestones of Japan–India relations (post World War II to the Cold War period)
1946–48: International Military Tribunal for the Far East (IMTFE), Justice Radhabinod Pal's 'Not guilty' verdict for defendants.
August 1947: India becomes an independent nation.
1949: PM Nehru gifts a baby elephant 'Indira' to Ueno Zoo.
April 1952: Establishment of Japan–India diplomatic relations.
1957: PM Nobusuke Kishi visits India, PM Nehru visits Japan.
1982: Start of Maruti Udyog Ltd., a joint venture between Suzuki and the Indian government.
1991: India's foreign exchange crisis and emergency loan from Japan.

2.6 RELIGIOUS AND SPIRITUAL BONDS; BUDDHAS AND VARIOUS GODS OF HINDUISM

Buddhism and Hinduism are siblings
Brahmanism was the predecessor of Hinduism. The current religious faith of over 80 per cent of Indians is Hinduism. Buddhism too emerged from Brahmanism. In other words, Buddhism and Hinduism are siblings.

Buddhism was transmitted to China and from there to Japan via Korea. The Japanese have always known that the roots of Buddhism are in India and have believed that Buddhas such as Mahavairocana, Amitabha, Shakyamuni, and Bhaisajyaguru (Healing Buddha) are believed to live in the Western paradise or 'Heaven' (India). India is the country that has had influence on the spiritual backbone of the Japanese people.

During the Nara period (710–94 CE), Emperor Shomu constructed the Todaiji Temple. When the ceremony to consecrate a newly-made Buddha statue by inserting the eyes (thereby investing it with soul) was held in 752 CE, among very high-ranking priests to preside over the ceremony was the Indian monk, Bodhisena, who had been invited from China where he was a highly respected monk.

Indians, whether Hindus, Muslims, or Buddhists, are all highly religious-minded. An embarrassing perception, though, is that Indians believe that Japanese are all devout Buddhists, which is not the case.

Buddhism was founded by Prince Siddhartha Gautama of the Shakya clan in the fifth century after he attained enlightenment following intense meditation and self-inflicted painful training. It was a reformative religion that came into being, because Brahmanism that was the dominant religion then had degenerated to lose its original light. Buddhism became a religion independent of Brahmanism, and yet inherited basic concepts such as reincarnation, karma (retributive justice), immortality of the soul, and so on.

Moreover, Hinduism that is prevalent today in India is an evolved form of Brahmanism as described in Chapter 1. Therefore, Hindus believe Buddhism as a religion is quite close to Hinduism. And many Hindus believe that Buddhism is a branch of Hinduism.

Hindu gods enshrined in Kyoto's Toji Temple (Temple of the East) and Sanjusangendo Temple (Temple with Outside Wall in Thirty-three Sections)

During his visit to Japan from late August to early September 2014, PM Modi visited Kyoto's Toji Temple (formally called Kyoo-gokokuji Temple) accompanied by PM Abe.

Why was it that PM Abe took PM Modi to this temple? Why was he not taken to the more popular Kiyomizu Temple or Kyoto Gozan (important temples of Kyoto including Nanzenji and Tenryuji)? The following is the author's guess, but he is quite confident about it.

Toji Temple was the first esoteric Buddhism temple built in 796 CE and later managed by Master Monk Kukai (popularly called Kobo-Taishi) based on the request of Emperor Saga. Kukai deepened his knowledge of Buddhism in China and back home started the 'Shingon Sect'. He constructed, as the centre of the sect, the Koyasan Sanctuary around Kongobuji Temple. In Toji Temple, one can understand the 'overall' state of Buddhism through the positioning of Buddha and the statues of other Buddhist deities housed in the Auditorium Hall. Here, the statues of five Buddhas and other deities of Buddhism and the statues of Hindu gods who were assigned the role of guarding the world of the Buddha have been enshrined.

In the Auditorium Hall of the Toji Temple, the Buddhas and various deities guarding them are positioned in accordance with the Buddhist hierarchy on a large pedestal, a simulation of Mount Sumeru. It is a sort of three-dimensional mandala (Buddhist visual scheme of the enlightened mind).

In the middle of the pedestal, a total of five wisdom Buddhas, namely Ratnasambhava, Amitabha, Amoghasiddhi, and Akshobhya with Mahavairocana at the centre are enshrined. Tathagata is the honorific title for a Buddha who has attained enlightenment. Surrounding them are enshrined five Bodhisattvas to the right (east side). Bodhisattva is a high-ranking monk-cum saviour before he has fully reached the state of Tathagata. And to the left (west side) on the opposite side are positioned five statues of Vidyaraja (wisdom kings) with Achalanatha (immovable protector) at the centre. Vidyaraja is a deity unique to esoteric Buddhism—it is the reincarnation of Tathagata to repel the devil.

On the eastern and western ends of the pedestal are the idols of Bonten and Taishakuten and on four corners of the pedestal are enshrined the Four Heavenly Kings who look strong and fierce guarding the four directions of the entire Sumeru pedestal. To the east is Jikokuten (Dhritarashtra), south is Zochoten (Virudhaka), west is Komokuten (Virupaksa), and north is Tamonten (Vaisravana). In case, Virupaksa is made and enshrined as an individual deity, it is called Bishamonten (armour-clad god of war); it is also known as Uesugi Kenshin (1530–78)—a powerful daimyo of the Sengoku period—worshipped him.

All in all, there are a total of twenty-one Buddhas and related statues in this hall. Mandala is known as the painting that depicts the world view of Buddhism, but at Toji Temple it is a three-dimensional mandala.

Buddhism deities with the Chinese character for 'heaven' attached to their names such as the 'Four Heavenly Kings', owe their origin to Hindu gods. Bonten, Taishakuten, and the Four Heavenly Kings in the Auditorium Hall of Toji temple are gods of Indian origin adopted in Buddhism.

Bonten is Brahma who is the creator of the universe in Hinduism and Taishakuten is Indra the god of thunder. Tamonten (also called Bishamonten) is Kubera or Vaisravana, the god of wealth. Other gods that are not enshrined in this temple but known to the Japanese are Bichuten or Naraenten (Vishnu) and Daijizaiten or Daikokuten (Shiva).

Kindly excuse the author for digressing yet again. The three leading gods of Hinduism, namely Brahma, Vishnu, and Shiva, have spouses (goddesses). They were also introduced in Japan along with their husbands. Saraswati, the wife of Brahma is Benzaiten (or Bensaiten), Lakshmi, the wife of Vishnu is Kisshoten, and Parvati, the wife of Shiva is Unmahi. Parvati is a powerful wife, and is known as the goddess that combats evils. When she gets angry, she would change herself to a fierce-looking Durga or Kali, but she is not much known in Japan. It is the author's conjecture that since she is too strong a goddess, perhaps she did not go down well with the Japanese mental frame of mind.

Moreover, in another hall, the Golden Hall of Toji Temple, idols of Yakushinyorai (Bhaisajyaguru), sunlight and moonlight Bodhisattvas and twelve divine generals are placed. These are also a must-see.

Another temple that depicts well the fusion of Buddhism and Hinduism is the Sanjusangendo Temple in Kyoto. It houses at the centre a big, seated statue of Senju Kannon

(Bodhisattva with 1,000 hands) and 500 smaller standing statues of Senju Kannon on the right side and a further 500 statues on the left side. Here, the noteworthy thing is that there are statues of Raijin (Varuna the Hindu god of water) on the extreme right, Fujin (Vayu the god of wind) on the extreme left and in between are twenty-eight guardian deities that trace their origin to Hinduism, standing in front. Among them one finds three leading gods of Hinduism, Taishakuten as well as Kisshoten. Senju Kannon, Raijin, and Fujin and other statues are categorized as national treasures as they are artistically and culturally top-class pieces of art. They are 'must-see' at the temple.

Varanasi and Sarnath, holy places for Buddhists and Hindus side by side

Based on the agreement of December 2015 on the prime ministers visiting each other every year alternately, PM Abe visited India. After the summit meeting at Delhi, PM Modi invited PM Abe to Varanasi (Benares) and he himself showed him around. Here, instead of 'Benares' (as the city is called in Japan) the author has decided to use 'Varanasi' that is close to the pronunciation in the native language.

Varanasi is the constituency of PM Modi. The visit to Varanasi was similar to PM Abe inviting Russian President Vladimir Putin to his native place in Yamaguchi in December 2016. It is quite common for the head of government to invite his counterpart to his native place. However, the real intention of PM Modi was to demonstrate to the people of both the countries and to international society the spiritual bond between Japan and India.

Varanasi is one of the holiest places of the Hindus. There is a belief that if Hindus take a bath in the Ganges flowing through Varanasi, all their sins up to that point are washed away. In addition, there is also a belief that after cremation, if the ashes are immersed in the Ganges, the soul is liberated from the karma of all previous births.

Sarnath is located on the outskirts of Varanasi. It is one of the top four holy places of Buddhism. These are Lumbini (in Nepal) the birthplace of Buddha, Bodh Gaya (Mahabodhi Temple, a World Heritage Site, is located here) where Buddha attained enlightenment, Sarnath where Buddha carried out his first sermon and Kushinagar where Buddha passed away (nirvana). At the time of the first sermon by Buddha in Sarnath, the legend goes that deer gathered around from the neighbouring forest and listened to the sermon along with Buddha's first disciples. That is why Sarnath is called Rokuyaon (meaning Deer Park) in Japan.

In this way, Varanasi is the common holy place for Buddhists and Hindus alike. It can indeed be said that Varanasi symbolizes the spiritual bond between Japan and India. That is why PM Modi chose to invite PM Abe over to this holy city.

3

THE METAMORPHOSIS OF INDIA

India is a cradle of one of the four great civilizations of the world together with Egypt, Mesopotamia, and China. Like the flow of the Ganges, India gives the impression of the eternal flow of time.

India is likened to an elephant, symbolizing the country's huge size with enormous strength, though moving slowly. On the other hand, China is likened to a dragon because the dragon is dynamic. The dragon can move freely in the sea and air and can even ascend to heaven.

The two most populous countries give the impression of being poles apart and just the opposite of each other. However, India is progressing steadily and gathering momentum in speed like an elephant that has set its goal and has started running.

Let's see what is India's goal? It is destined to become a global power. Since Independence, India is acknowledged as a leader of the Indian subcontinent. The Indian subcontinent comprises India, Pakistan, Bangladesh, Nepal, Bhutan, Sri Lanka, and the Maldives though the last two are not landlocked with the subcontinent. India was seen to be the sole big power in the region.

The objectives of India dramatically changed since the beginning of the 1990s. Its status started being projected as becoming elevated from a regional power to a global power.

In order to realize such a goal, first, India liberalized its state-controlled economic system by making a shift to a market-driven economy. Secondly, it swiftly improved its relationships with the advanced nations of the West with whom it had maintained a distance during the Cold War. And, thirdly, it built relationships with the nations of Asia–Pacific that are becoming the centre of gravity in the twenty-first century.

Japan can play a central role in all these areas.

3.1 FROM INDEPENDENCE TO THE END OF THE COLD WAR

Alienation from the West and Japan due to non-alignment
From World War II till the 1960s, not only India and Pakistan but the former colonies of Great Britain, France, Belgium, the Netherlands etc., in Asia, Africa, Central and South America got independence one after the other. They were not aligned to either of the two blocs; one led by capitalist America and the other by socialist Soviet Union and were politically called the Third World. Most of these former colonies were economically underdeveloped after years of exploitation by the colonial powers.

The countries belonging to the Third World disliked the Cold War confrontation between the two blocs premised on strong ideological differences. These liberated nations belonging to the Third World promoted the concept of non-alignment. PM Jawaharlal Nehru of India, President Sukarno of Indonesia, President Josip Broz Tito of Yugoslavia, and President Gamal Abdel Nasser of Egypt, considered as the fathers of independence in their respective countries, led this movement. PM Nehru in his speech in the Indian Parliament rejected military alliance and military blocs under the East–West Cold War confrontation. The majority of the countries that had gained independence in five continents during this intervening period expressed empathy with this new concept.

In Asia, PM Nehru reached out to the Chinese Premier Chou En-lai in 1954 for the first time. The talks resulted in the announcement of the Five Principles of Peaceful Coexistence, and these five principles became the backbone of non-alignment.

The Five Principles of Peaceful Coexistence were:

1. Mutual respect for each other's territorial integrity and sovereignty.
2. Mutual non-aggression.
3. Mutual non-interference in each other's internal affairs.
4. Equality and cooperation for mutual benefit.
5. Peaceful coexistence.

The heads of twenty-nine nations of Asia and Africa met in Bandung, Indonesia, in 1955 when the first Afro–Asian Conference was held. A '10-point declaration on the promotion of world peace and cooperation' based on the 'Five Principles of Peaceful Coexistence' was adopted. Incorporating the spirit of the UN Charter, it added such principles as respect for fundamental human rights, respect for the Charter of the United Nations, respect for the rights of individuals and collective defence, and prevention of big powers from resorting to collective defence.

The first Non-Aligned Movement (NAM) Conference was held in 1961. This conference had twenty-five members in the beginning, which gradually increased to 120 in 2016.

In this way, the Non-Aligned Movement demonstrated its existence during the Cold War in its own way. However, following China's aggression against India in 1962, China–India bilateral ties deteriorated. India started drifting more towards Russia as it (Russia) was a rival of China. The relevance of the Non-Aligned Movement came under question as a result.

3.2 FROM A NEWLY INDUSTRIALIZED COUNTRY TO A WORLD POWER

Birth of New India: breaking away from non-alignment

As the East–West confrontation disappeared with the collapse of the Berlin Wall in 1989, and subsequent disintegration of the Soviet Union, the Cold War came to an end. And, with that, the Non-Aligned Movement also lost its raison d'etre.

Here, India changed its course in a big way. Economically, it changed its policy from a Soviet style (or Chinese style) centrally controlled economy to a market-driven economy, leaving the economy to market forces. And politically, while maintaining its relationship with Russia, India strived to strengthen its relations with the leading western powers and Japan, among others. Its external policy has started to assume a global dimension. The policy of non-alignment constrained its option of warming up to major powers. That narrative changed; India opted to carve out a course to be a major power.

Towards the Asia-oriented 'Look East' policy and further to the 'Act East' policy

India launched the 'Look East' policy in the early 1990s to strengthen its relations with East Asia and Southeast Asia.

The reasoning was premised on the fact that under the banner of non-alignment during the Cold War, India was practically stuck with a Soviet-style planned and centrally controlled economy. On the contrary, East Asian countries had achieved remarkable growth. As a result, the gap with India had widened. East Asian countries and regions such as Japan, South Korea, Taiwan, Hong Kong, and China had rapidly progressed economically.

In addition, Southeast Asian countries followed them to also succeed in registering high economic growth. In 1967, Thailand, Indonesia, the Philippines, Malaysia, and Singapore came together to launch the Association of Southeast Asian Nations (ASEAN). Later, Brunei, Vietnam, Myanmar, Laos, and Cambodia joined the grouping to form a ten nation league.

The ten member nations of ASEAN put together had a population of 620 million in 2014, which made it bigger than the twenty-eight countries of EU put together. Their combined GDP in 2013 was US$2.4 trillion and was about half of that of Japan, making it the seventh largest in the world. Gradually, mutual ties among them were strengthened. In trade, free trade agreements (FTAs) were signed. Politically, their weight increased. The strength of the grouping was built with countries outside the region with ASEAN at the core. The ASEAN Charter was adopted in 2008 and the ASEAN Economic Community was established in 2015.

Indians tend to believe that Southeast Asia belongs to a greater Indian cultural sphere. Buddhism spread from India to Sri Lanka to reach Southeast Asia and Hinduism from South India to Southeast Asia. Buddhist temples and Buddhist fine arts spread to Myanmar, Thailand, Cambodia, and Laos and even today Buddhism is widespread there from the upper strata to the common masses. On the other hand, the influence of Hinduism is also strongly felt and traces of the Mahabharata and the Ramayana are to be found in ceremonies, sculptures temples, dances etc. The impact of Hinduism is particularly evident in Bali Island of Indonesia.

When the Malay Peninsula was a British colony, many Indian labourers were brought in to work in rubber and palm plantations. That is why, even today, 7 per cent and 9 per cent of the population of Malaysia and Singapore respectively is of Indian origin. Indian townships are to be found everywhere and Hindu temples are quite crowded. It was quite natural historically and emotionally for India to attach importance to its relations with Southeast Asian countries under the banner of the 'Look East' policy.

Thus, India entered the interactive system of dialogue with ASEAN in the latter half of the 1990s. Subsequently, on the recommendation and support of the Japanese PM Junichiro Koizumi, India also joined the East Asia Summit in 2005 along with Australia and New Zealand.

India had ample political and economic reasons for deepening its relations with ASEAN. The Modi government has taken the 'Look East' policy to the next level by rechristening it 'Act East' policy.

India goes global through BRICS and G20
In the twenty-first century India gained further weightage in the world. It had extricated itself from a regional power to emerge as a global power.

India formed BRICS with Brazil, Russia, China, and South Africa and became the leader of the so-called emerging countries, namely economically advanced nations among developing nations, thus gaining prominence in the international society.

BRICS got its name in 2001 based on a Goldman Sachs Report for investors. In the beginning, it was named BRICs referring to Brazil, Russia, India, and China—the final 's' stood for the plural form. These four countries met for the first time in 2009 in Yekaterinburg in Russia. In the BRICS Summit held in Beijing in 2011, South Africa joined the group and the small 's' became a capital 'S'.

India also joined the G20 Finance Ministers and Central Bank Governors Meeting and subsequently the G20 Summit. Thus, India became part of the Group of Twenty.

The G20 is the group that represents the advanced industrial economies of the world (G7) plus Russia (G8) and the leading countries of each continent. From the Asia–Pacific are Japan, China, India, Indonesia, South Korea, and Australia; from North America are America, Canada, and Mexico; from South America are Brazil and Argentina; from Europe are the UK, Germany, France, Italy, the EU, and Russia; from the Middle and Near East are Saudi Arabia and Turkey; and from Africa is South Africa. These twenty countries have held Finance Ministers and Central Bank Governors Meetings every year since 1999 to discuss financial and monetary problems. The G20 countries collectively account for nearly 90 per cent of world GDP and two-thirds of the world's population.

Here, I allow myself to deviate a bit.

I was the ambassador of Japan when the French President was Jacques René Chirac. He once remarked that the world from here on will neither be dominated by two countries, namely America and Russia, as during the Cold War period, nor the unipolar domination by America as in the post-Cold War period, but it ought to be a world managed and supported by representative capable countries from each continent. He called it a 'multipolar world'. And then, in the G8 Summit held at Évian, France, he extended invitations to representatives of the heads of government of G20 nations and the heads of leading international organizations such as the United Nations and the World Bank. Besides the member countries at its summit meeting, the G8 has the practice of inviting the heads of countries outside the region and holding talks with them. It is called the 'Outreach Meeting'. At Évian it was the first large-scale outreach meeting. In this outreach meeting of the G8, PM Koizumi of Japan too participated.

At the G8, it was only President Chirac who invited such a large number of countries from outside the region. At the Évian Summit, the author was to assist PM Koizumi as he was the Japanese Ambassador to France. From Lausanne in Switzerland which is on the opposite side of Lac Léman or Lake Geneva, the heads of states one after the other, took the ferry and crossed over to Évian. From the terrace of the hotel reserved for the summit, I saw the world leaders crossing the lake and gathering on the shore of scenic Évian. It was quite a spectacle.

In 2008, the first summit meeting of the G20 was held at Washington, D.C.—each country has the right to be chair of the summit by rotation.

One of the symbolic results of India's entry into the select band of world powers was the treatment of ambassadors of various countries accredited to India by the Ministry of External Affairs of India.

First, the handling of the National Day reception. Based on the international practice over many centuries and the Vienna Convention on Diplomatic Relations that defines the framework in this regard, the ambassador is the representative of the sending state and the recipient state (host nation in diplomatic terminology) must give courteous treatment to him/her. In every country, the ambassador incarnates the prestige of the sending state in the recipient state and acts to further friendship and goodwill with the latter. It is the general practice for the ambassador to hold a reception on the National Day of his/her country. In the case of Japan, the National Day is the emperor's birthday. Each country selects its National Day in accordance with their Constitution and other criteria.

The reception for the celebration of the emperor's birthday is hosted by the ambassador and his wife, and the representatives of various circles in the host nation, diplomatic corps, and Japanese expatriates are invited. It is usually held at the ambassador's residence but in case there is not enough space to accommodate the guests, it is held at a hotel. Since the birthday of Emperor Heisei falls on 23 December and overlaps with holidays such as Christmas, it is held at an earlier date. Otherwise many dignitaries would not be able to attend the reception.

It is an important matter and a matter of prestige for the sending state as well as the ambassador to personally receive dignitaries from the host state attending the reception, because it is an event that symbolizes the degree of friendship and importance attached to both the countries. However, it is very rare for the president, prime minister, or senior members of the royal family to attend this reception. While international protocol requires the host nation to treat every sending country equally, in principle, such busy dignitaries cannot physically attend receptions hosted by over a hundred ambassadors of sending countries. However, if they attend the reception of one country but not of the other without convincing reasons, it may become a sensitive issue on the part of the sending countries.

During the author's posting in India as the ambassador, the Indian government distinguished between the dignitaries who would be asked to attend such National Day receptions as representing the Indian government. For instance, the vice president, accompanied by his wife, attended receptions held by such world powers as the US, Japan, leading western nations, China etc., while in case of other countries, the lieutenant governor of Delhi attended with his wife. Both the vice president and the lieutenant governor are sent as representatives of the president.

In the reception for the emperor's birthday hosted by the author and his wife, the then Vice President Mr Krishan Kant and his spouse attended. Every year the vice president and his spouse would stand at the entrance of the big reception hall, next to the ambassador and his spouse, during the playing of the national anthems of both the countries; then, moving to the smaller reception room they would chat with the hosts, Indian dignitaries, head of the diplomatic corps (ambassador who has the longest duration in office), and the Japanese representatives of expatriates. Invitees whose number would run into the several hundred would chat in small groups in the huge lawn of the ambassador's residence enjoying drinks and buffet dinner.

However, since the last few years the level of participants as representatives of the Indian government has undergone certain changes and one cabinet minister is sent to the emperor's birthday reception, apparently by turn. It could perhaps be because the vice president has become busier compared to earlier, but it could also be because India has become a world power.

The reception at the Ministry of External Affairs varies from country to country. For Japan and other important countries, normally it is the foreign secretary, the top foreign service officer, who receives ambassadors, while ambassadors from other countries are received by secretary, east, or secretary, west. The world being carved out by the Ministry of External Affairs into east and west, broadly identifying the major parts of the world.

3.3 INDIA'S RELATION WITH CHINA—'NECKLACE OF PEARLS' STRATEGY AND 'DIAMOND STRATEGY'

Concerns around China's hegemony

China's expansionism, or, in the author's view, China's display of hegemonistic behaviour, is a matter of concern for neighbouring countries, who perceive it as a threat. It is not just political and economic expansionism. China is not shy of projecting power, and intends to be at par with America someday. Especially, China's power projection capability is already manifested in the Indo–Pacific region where its assertiveness is already on full display.

Perhaps Chinese President Xi Jinping's administration has apparently decided to discard the dictum of Deng Xiaoping to 'maintain a low profile till the opportune time'. Probably China has come to the conclusion that the 'time has come' to display its power.

China calls the maritime line extending from Japan to the Philippines as the first island chain and pretends that the East China Sea, South China Sea, and Taiwan belong to China's 'core interest'. In the East China Sea, despite having no credible historical evidence and disrespecting international law that does not support such claims, it has unilaterally enacted a law and staked its claim to the Senkaku Islands, which have been legitimately part of Japanese territory throughout history.

China continues to deploy its coast guard and even naval vessels around the Senkaku Islands almost on a daily basis in order to intimidate Japan and violates not only the contiguous zone of Japan but also the territorial sea, at times.

In the South China Sea, China has occupied, by force or threat, islands claimed by the Philippines, Vietnam, and Malaysia, as its territory. Besides, ignoring environmental concerns, it has converted coral reefs into man-made islands and has forcibly constructed airports, ports, and all kinds of structures. There are some facilities that are constructed mainly for military purposes.

In addition, crossing the first island chain, China is in the process of making inroads into the West Pacific. China regards the maritime line stretching from Japan to Guam as the second island chain. Its strategy is to arrest and prevent American forces from approaching the region from the west side in case of crisis. Today, Chinese naval vessels are engaged in threatening acts such as sailing to the West Pacific via the sea between Okinawa and Sakishima Islands or going around Taiwan. Some years ago, the Chinese deputy chief of naval staff remarked that the Pacific should be divided into East and West and that China should recognize American hegemony on the eastern side and that the western side, including Japan, should be entrusted to China. China seems to have unwavering resolve and a strategy and is gradually surging ahead to achieve its objective.

◆

EXPERIENCES FROM MY DAYS AS A DIPLOMAT (8)

VISITING BEIJING'S UNDERGROUND TUNNELS

In Article 7 of the Japan–China Joint Communique 1972, issued at the time of normalization of diplomatic relations between Japan and China, there is the following clause on anti-hegemony.

> The normalization of relations between Japan and China is not directed against any third country. Neither of the two countries should seek hegemony in the Asia–Pacific region and each is opposed to efforts by any other country or group of countries to establish such hegemony.

Further, during negotiations for the Treaty of Peace and Friendship between Japan and China concluded in 1978, China yet again strongly emphasized the inclusion of an 'anti-hegemony clause' in the treaty. Those days, China felt the threat of Soviet Union hegemony and tried to counter it along with Japan.

Since the author was working as First Secretary in the Japanese Embassy in Beijing towards the end of the Cultural Revolution from 1974 to 1976, he is one of the living witnesses to China's anti-hegemony policy.

At that time, an extensive underground network of tunnels was spread across Beijing like the mesh of a net. Besides serving as shelters in the event of Soviet attacks, they were also to serve as bases for guerilla warfare in case the Soviet Union invaded China. Chairman Mao Zedong used to boast that China would win using guerilla warfare if the Soviet Union invaded China.

Readers may not believe this, but the author along with his wife, was permitted to go down and see the underground tunnels in Beijing. Those days there was no source of entertainment in China. There were hardly a dozen restaurants where foreigners could go for dining, and yet the Chinese government willingly invited them to see the underground tunnels and their preparedness against any invasion. The entrance to these tunnels was from inside sundry daily shops and other buildings. As we went down, we could see food reserves at many places inside the long tunnels. The reason for taking Japanese diplomats to see the tunnels was to publicize the threat of the Soviet Union and at the same time hope to counter it through Japan–China cooperation.

It was remarkable that China which wanted an anti-hegemony clause to be included in earlier treaties is now practising hegemony itself. This turnaround of Chinese attitudes was ironic

Negotiations for the Treaty of Peace and Friendship between Japan and China were not easy and Japan had to accommodate China's requests to make that possible.

Article 2 of the Treaty of Peace and Friendship between Japan and China signed in 1978 reiterates Article 7 of the Joint Communique of 1972 and stipulates as follows.

> The Contracting Parties declare that neither of them should seek hegemony in the Asia–Pacific region or in any other region and that each is opposed to efforts by any other country or group of countries to establish such hegemony.

◆

China's 'One Belt One Road' initiative and India

China is also in the process of making inroads into the Indian Ocean. India's geopolitical importance is due to its location. It is located in the southern part of central Eurasia and protrudes into the Indian Ocean. India is surrounded by the Bay of Bengal in the east, Indian Ocean in the south, and the Arabian Sea in the west. If one stands at Cape Comorin (in India, it is called Kanyakumari, a Hindu holy place), at the southernmost point of the subcontinent, one can clearly see the three water bodies in three different colours where they meet. Off Cape Comorin runs the long and wide sea lane from the Strait of Malacca to Africa, on one hand, and the Strait of Hormuz at the entry point of the Persian Gulf, on the other.

Since the Himalayas are located in the north of India, China cannot directly access the Indian Ocean by a land route. Thus, it has to be either through Myanmar in the east or Pakistan in the west.

The president of China, Xi Jinping, talked about 'The China Dream'.

First of all, he talked of consolidating the neighbourhood. In order to make the South Sea of China as the 'China Sea', China has ignored the territorial claims of Southeast Asian countries to the surrounding islands, occupied them with military power in the background, and is constructing various facilities that are also meant for military use. Its strategy is to bring the neighbouring countries under Chinese influence. His dream has a strong resemblance to the former 'Chinese Tributary System' under which neighbouring countries paid tributes to China. Next, he talked of expanding the influence of China.

It is called 'The Belt and Road Initiative'. It is a strategy to develop both land and sea routes up to Europe and along with securing access to Europe, put the countries en route under the influence of China. The land route is the road to Europe via Central Asia along the old Silk Route, while the sea route connects China with Europe and Africa via the Indian Ocean and the Suez Canal. Already Chinese companies have acquired partial rights for Athens port in Greece.

As for 'The Belt', it must pass through the countries of Central Asia and the Caucasus. If these countries feel that strengthening relations with China would be useful for them, they will cooperate. However, under the name of 'Great Eurasianism', Russia is trying to restore close links with these countries, even if not at the same level as it was during the Soviet Union age. Russia will not remain indifferent to these countries coming under the Chinese sphere of influence.

It will be the Indian Ocean that will be the 'route'. Thus, China's 'One Belt One Road Initiative' is a matter of great concern for India.

China is strengthening its navy in order to have a powerful ocean fleet. At the time of writing this manuscript, a second-hand aircraft carrier 'Liaoning' of Soviet design, that China acquired from Ukraine has been commissioned into regular service and China is building one more aircraft carrier. It also must be planning to create multiple task forces led by carriers. Part of these ocean fleets will exercise influence from the South China Sea to the West Pacific and its objective is to counter American forces crossing outside the second island chain in case of any crisis. The other objective is meant for the Indian Ocean.

China has supported the construction of Sittwe Port in Myanmar, Chittagong Port in Bangladesh, Hambantota Port in Sri Lanka, and Gwadar Port in Pakistan, using abundant funds and Chinese labour brought from the homeland. On the surface, China says that these are meant to be commercial ports to develop trade for these countries, but it is rumoured that someday they will be used as ports of call to refuel Chinese ocean fleets. A Chinese submarine has already called on Sri Lanka's Hambantota Port and has rubbed India the wrong way. China has expanded its interests in the Hambantota Port. However, Sri Lanka which has borrowed huge funds from China for the construction of the port is in a tight financial situation, so much so that Sri Lanka was obliged to concede to China a ninety-nine-year lease of the port.

If these four ports are connected, they will encircle India. Someone has given it a well-thought-out name—'String of Pearls'. It is a strategy to put a noose around India's neck.

In addition, China is also developing land routes to the Indian Ocean. One route provides access to the Bay of Bengal from Yunnan province by going down south from the Irrawaddy River in Myanmar. Another one is the road to friendly Pakistan crossing the Karakoram Range. If these two roads, especially the latter one, get developed, China will secure the shortest access route to the Persian Gulf and the Suez Canal. The latter route, if completed, will be called the China–Pakistan Economic Corridor (CPEC). Thus, even if the US and other countries control the Strait of Malacca, China will have access to the Indian Ocean.

The sea lane from the Strait of Malacca to the Persian Gulf or the Suez Canal via the Indian Ocean is the lifeline for the economies of many Asian countries, including Japan. Maritime trade, especially crude and natural gas from the Middle East are strategically important not only for Japan but for other nations as well. If China does not adopt a peaceful stance and enhances its maritime footprint in the Indian Ocean, one would have reasons to worry.

At present, the security in the Indian Ocean is being guaranteed by the Indian Navy and the United States Seventh Fleet. It needs no explanation to show how significant it is for Japan that India, a great pro-Japan country, and the Seventh Fleet of America, an ally, are safeguarding this sea lane, thereby protecting Japan's economic interests.

India's love–hate relationship with China

On the surface, India seems to maintain friendly bilateral relations with China. Despite differences on bilateral issues, both hold a common stance when it comes to taking a position on issues vis-à-vis the advanced nations. For example, both put up a combined defence in most of the cases against the proactive demand of advanced nations in fora on climate change, multilateral trade liberalization by the WTO or the Regional Comprehensive Economic Partnership (RCEP), and so on. India and China also work in unison in BRICS and both have jointly led the inception of the BRICS Bank. India was one of the first countries to join the Asian Infrastructure Investment Bank (AIIB) which was established based on a Chinese concept and initiative. On the trade front, though India has a huge trade deficit with China, it still reaps economic benefits from trading with China.

Notwithstanding the complementarity on the economic front, both have sharp differences and opposing stances on territorial and security issues. India has faced military infiltrations by China on many occasions in the past. In particular, China's military invasion by crossing the Himalayas in 1962 resulted in an Indo–China war and ended with India's partial defeat. This experience still rankles India. It is a trauma from which India is yet to recover.

As a result of the Indo–China War of 1962, China continues to occupy the Aksai Chin area in Kashmir, which is India's territory. In the Ladakh region in the north-west Himalayas that is India's territory, too, China has been infiltrating from time to time. However, each time India has successfully driven back the Chinese troops. This has not deterred China from claiming Arunachal Pradesh in India's Northeast Himalayan region as its own territory. When the author was posted in India, the Asian Development Bank (ADB) wanted to finance a power project in Arunachal Pradesh, but China opposed it on the ground that it is disputed territory between India and China. In the border area of Arunachal Pradesh and Tibet, the Chinese army infiltrates from time to time even now.

India–China bilateral issues are not only confined to territorial issues. Even in the political domain, China has tried to put India in a corner. For example, despite India's credentials, China stubbornly opposes India's entry into the Nuclear Suppliers Group (NSG), despite all the other forty-seven members, including Japan, supporting India. With consensus continuing to remain elusive, India is unable to join the group. Even with regard to the United Nations Security Council (UNSC) reform (see Chapter 4) being pursued by Japan and India (plus Germany and Brazil), China continues to oppose it. And, above all, the perceived security threat from China such as the Chinese support to Pakistan, a constant threat for India in the form of cross-border terrorism from Pakistan and China's advance into the Indian Ocean loom large over India and adversely impact bilateral ties.

Meaning of 'strategic autonomy'
Perhaps because India still has the vestiges of the DNA of non-alignment, its public stance is that it does not seek to enter into a formal alliance with any country and prefers to remain fiercely independent without any foreign baggage. India has especially good relations with Russia and the weapons used by the Indian armed forces are mostly imported from Russia. However, India does not construe this as an alliance. Though India's relationship with the US has warmed and both even hold joint military exercises in the Indian Ocean, India pretends not to seem to have an alliance partnership with America.

The strategic and security community in India calls such a stance or policy as 'strategic autonomy'. On the surface, it could appear to be another version of non-alignment but there is a difference. Such a stance could be premised on the fact that though India is against entering into any military alliance with a particular country, the maintenance of nuclear deterrents constitutes a key element of national policy to deter any external threat, perceived or real. Though India does not enter into any alliance, India prefers to strengthen its relations with western powers, especially with the US.

Its nuclear programme was demonstrated by the nuclear tests it conducted in 1998. Even with regard to missiles, it is gradually extending their range and power and is devoted to the development of mid-range ballistic missiles that can reach the heart of China. Even if China launches a nuclear attack first, in order to be able to retaliate with nuclear weapons, India is not only developing land-based nuclear bombs but also nuclear missiles that can be launched from submarines.

However, with China's military might gathering steam and posing a potentially big threat in the Indian Ocean, it will be difficult for India to manage its security by itself. Such a strategic consideration has led to a rethinking of the so-called 'strategic autonomy'. As a result, India has started attaching a lot of importance to its relations with the US. Attaching increased importance to Japan, an ally of America, also seems to be a part of this new strategy.

The Indian Ocean falls under the jurisdiction of the United States Seventh Fleet with its headquarters in Hawaii. It covers the sea from the West Pacific to the Indian Ocean. One of the bases of the Seventh Fleet is located in Diego Garcia in the Indian Ocean. This island is a British facility leased to America. Recently, in view of Chinese incursions in the Indian Ocean, India and the US have launched joint naval exercises named the Malabar Manoeuvres. More recently, the US and India have invited Japan's SDF for the same exercises on a regular basis and the same has been institutionalized. Thus, the US, India, and Japan have come together in the maritime domain and are holding joint exercises with a view to deterring Chinese advance in the Indian Ocean region.

Australia is also cautious about China's increasing involvement through economic assistance to island nations of the South Pacific. China has also acquired interests in Darwin Port in northern Australia. Australia also faces the Indian Ocean.

Australia and India are leading members of the Indian Ocean Rim Association (IORA), established in 1995. Japan and India have already agreed to invite Australia for the policy dialogues. In the future, if military cooperation between Australia and India over the Indian Ocean deepens, it will be possible to link four vertices namely, Japan, the US (Hawaii), Australia, and India and realize the 'Diamond (Rhombus) Cooperation'.

3.4 INDIA'S PRESENCE AND COMMUNICATION CAPABILITY IN INTERNATIONAL SOCIETY

India's ability to communicate and impress international society is quite big. And India's presence in international society in proportion to its economic growth is equally noticeable.

There are several factors behind this, but the foremost contribution to India's standing in international society comes from the Indian diaspora. Their number is said to be in excess of 30 million and they are spread over Europe and America, Southeast Asia, the Middle and Near East, and East and South Africa. Earlier they were called Indian merchants abroad but today they are not necessarily engaged in trade any more. They have forayed into other fields in recent times. In the advanced nations, they are active in a wide range of fields such as IT, finance, medicine, law, and so on. There are many who also head global MNCs. Satya Nadella, CEO of Microsoft, Nitin Nohria, Dean of Harvard Business School, for example, are globally well-known names. There are many others the world over in well-placed positions as well.

Some of the diaspora communities have also entered politics in the countries of their adoption. For example, some of those who acquired citizenship of America after migration have joined politics and their number is increasing steadily. Out of the fifty states that constitute the United States of America, the former governor of South Carolina, Nikki Haley, and the former governor of Louisiana, Piyush 'Bobby' Jindal, are Americans of Indian origin. Nikki Haley was appointed as the United States Ambassador to the United Nations by former President Donald Trump. In the most recent US administration, Vice President Kamala Harris is partially of Indian origin.

There is a US–India Friendship Parliamentary League called the Congressional Caucus on India and Indian Americans in the US Congress and this organization has about 200 registered congressional members from both the houses.

Similarly, the presence of Indians in Europe, especially in the UK, the former colonial power, is equally strong. India was a victim of exploitation at the hands of the East India Company since the seventeenth century and was a colony of Great Britain, called the 'British Raj' between 1858 and 1947. Before the advent of British rule, India was under the Mughals with the centre of power resting in the northern part of the country. With the decline of the Mughals, Great

Britain overthrew the Mughal empire in 1858 by banishing the last Muslim emperor, Bahadur Shah Zafar, to Burma and colonized India by appointing a viceroy as the representative of the monarch of England. After India achieved Independence, both the UK and India have a kind of love-hate relationship. However, residents in the UK from the former British Raj (including Pakistan) have increased thanks to easier immigration policies applied to those from erstwhile British colonies. In recent years, Indians are increasing in numbers in other EU countries as well.

However, in June 2016, the UK decided to withdraw from the EU (Brexit) based on a national referendum and after several discussions and negotiations, at the end of January 2020, the UK finally left the EU. The biggest trigger for such a move was to put a stop to increasing numbers of immigrants and refugees.

Today, Indians are migrating to the US and Canada in large numbers and many Indians travel to these countries for trade and higher studies. Earlier, Indians travelled to America and Canada westwards via London. However, today, thanks to India's relations with the West Coast of US and Canada, many Indians travel eastwards via Japan. Three airlines namely, Japan Airlines, All Nippon Airways, and Air India operate direct flights between Japan and India and the majority of passengers are Indians. Their final destination is not always Japan but the US or Canada via Narita.

In the Middle East, a large number of Indian labourers work in the Gulf countries. In recent years, they are no longer employed only as cheap labour but are active in government and governmental organizations and at higher levels in private companies.

Owing to the geographical proximity of East and South

Africa to India, Indians and people of Indian origin occupy influential positions in these countries.

There are many Indians who have excelled in international organizations including the United Nations and the percentage of Indians who serve in these organizations is much higher than the financial contribution or the contribution ratio of India. Indians have demonstrated the capacity to survive in a highly competitive world. It is in direct contrast to Japan's relatively poor performance in terms of staff of the United Nations, especially at the senior level, despite Japan being number two in the world in terms of financial contributions to international organizations.

4

ECONOMIC AND BUSINESS COOPERATION

4.1 NATION-BUILDING AND ENHANCING THE PRESENCE OF JAPAN IN INDIA

Human resource development through the ODA

Japan has been extending cooperation to India for nation-building and human resource development since 1958. The history and scale of this cooperation is long and large. Cooperation with Japan is highly valued and appreciated by the Indian government. It is matched equally by public admiration. Based on past achievements, the projection for the future also looks good. The most powerful tool for this economic cooperation is the commitment and disbursement of Official Development Assistance (ODA) by Japan.

According to the 'White Paper on ODA' published by the Ministry of Foreign Affairs, Japan, the ultimate goal of Japan's ODA to India is 'cooperation for the realization of more inclusive and sustainable development of India based on the common values of Japan and India'.

The three mid-term goals are as follows:

1. Enhancing connectivity.
2. Strengthening industrial competitiveness.
3. Supporting inclusive and sustainable growth.

Enhancing connectivity

Enhancing connectivity means the development of connectivity at the national and regional level, or to be more precise, development and improvement of transport and traffic networks and means of communication as well as simplification of customs clearance and immigration procedures. It is aimed at strengthening friendly and economic ties between the two countries by facilitating the easy movement and revitalization of goods, services, and people.

The White Paper on the ODA of the Japanese government goes as follows:

> Bearing in mind the elimination of bottlenecks on the infrastructure front for investment and growth, and in order to enhance connectivity between leading industrial towns, within economic zones and between regions in India, Japan extends support for the development of transportation infrastructure which would become hubs and networks and the power infrastructure, for example railways (including high speed railways and metro), national highways (including expressways), power and other basic infrastructure projects. In addition, Japan promotes realization of wide-area economic development such as the Delhi–Mumbai Industrial Corridor (DMIC) and the Chennai–Bengaluru Industrial Corridor (CBIC). Further, Japan extends cooperation for the enhancement of connectivity in the Northeast region of India, as agreed in the Japan–India Summit.

Japanese yen loans mostly target infrastructure development in fields such as power (construction of power generation plants and development of transmission and distribution network) that would require a large amount of finance. In addition, there are projects related to water and sewer services and afforestation. But India accords top priority to projects that help secure connectivity across such a vast country.

Transforming India's urban transport through Japanese style metro system

The path-breaking programme in the Japanese ODA-based support to India is the construction of the metro system (urban transport network centred on the metro) in metropolitan cities starting with Delhi. In the metro system, Japanese style management systems, software, and operations equipment (partly manufactured overseas) have been used. On-time arrival and departure operations, orderly queuing up for boarding, cleanliness, exclusive compartment for ladies etc., are all modelled in the Japanese style.

When the author was posted in India, one day Dr E. Sreedharan, Managing Director of Delhi Metro Rail Corporation, came to him for consultation. It was about the proposal of the Indian Railways and the Ministry of Railways to make joint use of tracks of the National Railways and the incoming Delhi Metro for thorough service for both the systems. Dr Sreedharan's concern was that if he agreed to it, the well-known maladies of Indian Railways would infiltrate into the Delhi Metro system. If allowed, the new system that he was trying to create with so much effort and passion would come to naught and he wanted the author's cooperation in this regard. Indian Railways suffers from a plethora of problems such as frequent delays, unclean trains and stations, ticketless travel, rampant crime on the trains etc. The Delhi Metro was planned as an independent system totally divorced from Indian Railways. Therefore, the author also approached the Indian Railways along with Dr Sreedharan to make sure of the success of the Delhi Metro.

Prior to this, the author had heard that the coaches for Delhi Metro would be ordered from South Korea because of cheaper prices and felt that it was something unacceptable to Japan. The author visited the ministries of finance and railways and made them agree to at least use equipment such as Japanese motors and other vital equipment, which are key components of engines.

Even today, the expansion of the Delhi Metro network continues with new lines or extension of existing lines being constructed. The Delhi Metro is not only contributing to easing traffic congestion but is also helping in curbing environmental pollution. Inspired by the success story of the Delhi Metro, many Indian cities are trying to replicate it. Metro construction has spread to metropolitan cities such as Mumbai, Chennai, Bengaluru, Hyderabad, Jaipur, and Cochin. Kolkata already had a system supported by Japan which is also being expanded now. Japanese ODA funding has been extended to some of the metros of these cities.

According to the author, the success of metro projects has given self-confidence to Indians that they can also do it (like Japan). It is a 'revolutionary' project that has kindled the 'can do' spirit among Indians and enhanced their self-respect and confidence.

Cooperation with the Indian Railways

Despite many shortcomings, demonizing the Indian Railways is not appropriate. Japan has contributed to Indian Railways also in a big way.

The history of Indian Railways dates back to British colonial rule. The total length of Indian Railways is one of the world's largest. However, the quality is not very good. Equipment, technology, and service do not compare with those of Japan.

Delays are a routine affair. Due to poor maintenance, train derailment is quite frequent. The main stations are big but trespassers on station premises are to be found everywhere. At times, there are foul smells floating around. Ticketless travel is also rampant. Many readers must have seen images of passengers in clusters on the ramp or rooftop of a train. As a safeguard against ticketless travellers or deboarding through the window, there are grills on the window. As a result, in the event of an accident, passengers are unable to escape through the window, resulting in tragedies.

The size of India's railway budget is extremely big. Until 2016, there used to be a separate budget for railways from the General Budget, but since the financial year (FY) 2017 the two have been merged by the Modi government. However, funds always fall short of the ever-growing demand. In addition, Indian Railways is a 'golden goose that lays golden eggs' for Indian politicians. The post of railway minister is thus an object of envy for politicians. They build stations in their constituencies and make them regular halts for express trains.

Japan, too, had a similar situation during the period when the railways were nationalized. Since the privatization in 1987 of the Japan National Railways into six Japan Railways (JR) companies—five regional companies, JR Hokkaido, JR East, JR Tokai, JR West, JR Kyushu, and one freight company—the quality and speed of improvement of railway systems have seen a remarkable transformation. The magnitude of problems in Indian National Railways is of a different and more serious level compared to that in Japan.

In view of such a situation and to improve Indian Railways, Japan has been extending technical support to Indian Railways and the Ministry of Railways for a long time.

In the Indian Railways network, the most important line

in terms of economic importance is the one connecting the capital, Delhi, with the financial capital, Mumbai. Another important line is the one connecting Delhi with Kolkata. While the former is called the Western Corridor, the latter is the Eastern Corridor. These two lines are the main arteries of India. Since passenger trains and freight trains share the same tracks, it is the main reason behind frequent delays for both.

Therefore, the Indian government launched the initiative of doubling the lines with separate ones for passengers and for freight. Japan was selected for the construction of a dedicated freight railway line in the Western Corridor having a length of about 1,500 kilometres. Many years of cooperation by Japan Railways, one of the best in the world, has clinched it for Japan.

Both the governments named this plan as the Dedicated Freight Corridor (DFC) and jointly promoted the construction project. It is a comprehensive, large-scale project that involves all kinds of financial cooperation, namely ODA from the Japanese government, non-ODA financial cooperation from Japan Bank for International Cooperation (JBIC) as well as private banks, and overall technical cooperation from the Japan International Cooperation Agency (JICA) and JR Freight Railway Company. A large number of Japanese companies including many trading companies are engaged in the project. The yen loan amount for this project will perhaps surpass the total yen loans extended to India till date.

Japanese shinkansen (bullet train) to run in India
At present, there is no high speed railway (HSR) in India. If anyone wants to travel the vast expanse of India, one has to either travel by train which takes several days or travel by the expensive air network. As of now, the Indian government has planned for six HSR routes and has asked various foreign

countries for feasibility studies. Among them, a decision on the 500 kilometre long Mumbai–Ahmedabad route was taken quite early and Japanese cooperation was sought. Following the feasibility study by JICA, both the governments agreed to induct Japanese shinkansen on this route. PM Modi, a great friend of Japan, coming to power also played a big role in this regard. JR East is extending full cooperation for this project. Besides yen loans, there is financial cooperation also from other sources in Japan for this project.

During PM Modi's visit to Japan in November 2016, PM Abe himself took a ride with PM Modi in the shinkansen and took him to the shinkansen coach plant of the Kawasaki Heavy Industry in Kobe. A shinkansen coach plant will also be established in India based on Japanese cooperation.

Japan was slighted when China bagged the Jakarta–Bandung high speed railway project in Indonesia. India's shinkansen project proved to be a counterpoint for Japan as it had lost the Indonesia project to China. This project in Indonesia is not making much headway due to issues with land acquisition and other problems. On the contrary, the project in India will perhaps progress smoothly, as besides the Indian government and Indian Railways, there is overall cooperation in terms of funds and technology from the Japanese government, JICA, JBIC, and related companies in Japan.

If this project is successfully implemented, there are chances of Japanese shinkansen getting adopted on other routes as well because it would be highly uneconomical to have Japanese style shinkansen on the Mumbai–Ahmedabad route and the French TGV on other routes, for example. China is also aiming to enter the Indian HSR market, but the Indian side knows very well that what Chinese claim to be 'Made in China' technology and systems is actually a copy of foreign technology including that of Japan. In addition, India will be wary of involving China in such projects because of its long-standing and unresolved territorial disputes with China as well as China's advance into the Indian Ocean. The Indian government and the people are also perhaps of the view that however cheap the Chinese offer may be, it is not welcome as Chinese intentions are always suspect.

Development of Northeast India and enhancing connectivity with Southeast Asia

The seven states in Northeast India are economically underdeveloped. They are Arunachal Pradesh, Assam, Manipur, Meghalaya, Mizoram, Nagaland, and Tripura. The land route from the rest India to the Northeast along the north of Bangladesh is a narrow corridor, called the Siliguri Corridor, also known as the Chicken's Neck. All the seven states are eagerly waiting for the development of this corridor that connects them with West Bengal. In addition, these seven states are also considering establishing access with ASEAN countries via their neighbour, Myanmar. Northeast India had close relations with Japan due to the Battle of Imphal. The remains of Japanese soldiers are still being found here. Myanmar has been a great friend of Japan through vicissitudes and Japan's cooperation with that country has been progressing well. Therefore, there is no better candidate than Japan to connect Northeast India with Myanmar.

In this way, PM Modi and PM Abe have agreed on cooperation for rail and road connectivity between Northeast India and Myanmar. Although the project is at an early stage, when complete, along with the sea route from Chennai to ASEAN, a circle of connectivity will be completed around the Bay of Bengal.

Main projects of Japan–India Economic Cooperation

- **Economic cooperation with India**

  Next-generation infrastructure, connectivity, transport system, smart cities, rejuvenation of the Ganges and other rivers, manufacturing, clean energy, skill development, water security, food processing, agro-industry, agriculture cold chain, and rural development (Japan–India Summit talks, September 2014).

- **Dedicated Freight Corridor (DFC) project**

  The DFC project in the Western Corridor (Delhi–Mumbai) that accounts for 60 per cent of total freight traffic and the Eastern Corridor (Delhi–Kolkata). Japan is extending support for the Western Corridor. Japan started disbursing yen loans in October 2009 and the total loan disbursed till March 2013 is worth ¥230.6 billion.

- **The DMIC initiative**

  The DMIC initiative envisages wide area development in six states—National Capital Region, Uttar Pradesh, Haryana, Rajasthan, Madhya Pradesh, and Maharashtra—along with the DFC in order to develop twenty-four clusters consisting of manufacturing factories, industrial townships, power plants, logistic centres between Delhi and Mumbai. This initiative has been promoted since 2006. The Japanese side has announced contribution of fund facilitation to the tune of US$4.5 billion.

- **Chennai–Bengaluru Industrial Corridor (CBIC) initiative**

  The CBIC initiative project is similar to the DMIC and plans infrastructure development between the Chennai and Bengaluru region where many Japanese companies, including automobile manufacturers, are present.

- **High speed railways initiative**
  Joint implementation of the Mumbai–Ahmedabad route by Japan and India as mentioned above.
- **The development of Northeast India and enhancement of connectivity with ASEAN**
  Agreement on cooperation for infrastructure building in Northeast India to improve connectivity between India and ASEAN, with Myanmar as the gateway, as mentioned earlier.

Strengthening the industrial competitiveness of India
The White Paper on the ODA of Japan describes the second ODA policy to India as follows.

> Strengthening industrial competitiveness, especially in the field of manufacturing, is the key to make Indian economic growth more stable. Manufacturing industry generates new employment for the young productive population, strengthens technological base of the economy, and enhances productivity. Based on such perspective, Japan shall extend support for the development of important infrastructure such as power generation, transmission and distribution, improvement in energy efficiency, high standard roads, ports, water and sewage etc., that contribute to strengthening of industrial competitiveness of India, including manufacturing. In addition, Japan shall extend support that contributes to promotion of foreign direct investment (FDI) in India and development of industrial human resource in fields such as management, higher education and technical skills to put plans into practice.

It is obvious from the above that the focus of Japanese ODA to India is cooperation in the area of manufacturing industry and infrastructure development.

The former matches with PM Modi's policies 'Make in India' and 'Skill India' that are close to his heart. Nearly 60 per cent of India's population is engaged in agriculture, and yet the growth of the manufacturing industry is essential for India's economic growth and employment generation. Though India has a strong base in the IT industry, and has made rapid strides, its contribution to industrial capability and employment generation is relatively small. There are industries such as pharmaceuticals, iron, steel, and oil refineries in India, but for India's size they are not enough. Increase in investment from overseas is also necessary for industrial promotion. Besides helping India in this regard, Japanese ODA has cooperated with India in human resource development through technical cooperation such as the training of Indian engineers. Japanese experts have been sent to India to enable the development of technical skills. The entry of Suzuki Company into India ushered in a kind of revolution in the automobile industry and has been a trendsetter for other industries to move in to create a win-win situation.

Be that as it may, India still lags behind in infrastructure development. Power plants and the transmission and distribution of power, railways, roads, ports, water, sewage services etc., are not being able to meet the demand and they are hampering India's economic growth. Thus, there is infinite scope for Japanese cooperation with India.

Far-reaching industrial corridor initiatives

The aim of the Delhi–Mumbai Industrial Corridor that passes through six states between Delhi and Mumbai is to construct four industrial townships or clusters (two big and two small) in each state. They are supposed to become the hubs for industry, commerce, and distribution in the six states of

National Capital Region, Uttar Pradesh, Haryana, Rajasthan, Gujarat, Madhya Pradesh, and Maharashtra. These clusters will be constructed along the aforesaid freight corridor (DFC). In addition, there will be six smart cities along this industrial corridor, all self-sustaining in terms of education, power, housing, law and order, malls, restaurants etc. Leading Japanese companies such as Toshiba, Hitachi, and NEC will participate in the development of smart cities. The Indian government intends to encourage healthy competition among these six cities.

A similar industrial corridor is being planned between Chennai and Bengaluru. It is called the Chennai–Bengaluru Industrial Corridor (CBIC). It is a welcome project for Japan, as the number of Japanese companies entering South India continues to increase.

In March 2017, the author was surprised when he visited President Amitabh Kant of the corporation responsible for the DMIC, who told the author that three other industrial corridors, similar to the DMIC and CBIC, are being planned. One was the industrial corridor from Kolkata to Amritsar in Punjab via Delhi and the second was from Kolkata to Chennai along the Bay of Bengal. The third was from Mumbai to Bengaluru via Pune. If these three are connected to the DMIC and CBIC, it will create a circular industrial corridor encircling the whole of India. Therefore, a pan-India industrial corridor corporation, that looks after all the five industrial corridors, has been established, he was told.

India's infrastructure is, on the whole, relatively poor. Therefore, the Indian government and state governments are earnestly promoting the development of infrastructure and the construction of industrial townships where certain tax incentives will be offered. Several industrial townships exclusively for Japanese companies based on the cooperation of the Japanese government and companies are also being developed. States like Delhi, Haryana, Rajasthan, Karnataka, Tamil Nadu, and Andhra Pradesh are quite keen to attract Japanese companies to their respective states. With a view to revitalizing the local economy, these states are pursuing the development of industrial townships in partnership with the Japanese government and companies, offering preferential support measures such as tax exemption and making land available for such projects.

Japan–India investment promotion partnership

During PM Modi's visit to Japan in September 2014, PM Abe and PM Modi signed a joint declaration in which ¥3.5 trillion of fresh public and private investment and financing from Japan in five years was promised. The Indian side agreed to improve the investment environment in India to facilitate investment by Japan by promoting a 'Special Package for Japanese Investment'. Its objective was to promote investment by Japanese companies in India.

There are, however, certain difficulties in the investment climate in India.

The foremost is power scarcity. Except for some regions (such as Gujarat and the vicinity of Chennai), foreign companies by and large face power shortages. Power breakdown and voltage fluctuations are a daily affair. In addition to power generation shortage, the foremost reasons are shoddy power grids where there is loss of power during transmission and power theft as factories and households steal electricity. Foreign companies are obliged to install captive power generation facilities in their factories to deal with power breakdowns. This is obviously unwanted extra investment. Most of the households have given up on getting uninterrupted power, while the affluent class and foreigners install power gensets in their homes.

Indian roads are also of poor quality. Expressways in the real sense of the term are very few in number such as the Delhi–Agra Expressway, Mumbai–Pune Expressway, and the Bandra–Worli Sea Link in Mumbai.

National highways are, on the whole, in poor shape. In addition to cars and trucks, one can find even bullock carts and carts pulled by camels on the same roads. Thus, these roads are extremely dangerous and accident prone.

When the author was staying in India, one of the Japanese companies making sheet glass with its factory in Gurugram complained that many of the glass shipments break on NH 8 during transportation. Maruti Suzuki that has factories in Gurugram and Manesar is also apprehensive about safe transport when it sends its cars on trucks. The DMIC will be a solution to this problem.

Drinking water and sewage systems are also a problem in India. Drinking water cannot be consumed without boiling and sterilization. Yet heavy metals cannot be isolated. In India, the majority of areas have no drinking water supply. Securing industrial water is also a source of headache. Access to water is a struggle for both companies as well as individuals.

In rural areas, as ground water is drawn excessively for agriculture, there is the intrusion of salty water. When the water evaporates, the ground covered with salt hampers cultivation. India has inadequate energy resources but the water shortage is really acute.

India's sewage system is also poor. The Yamuna, a tributary of the Ganges, that flows through Delhi, is a holy river, but if one goes close, one finds sewage effluents and all kinds of objects floating in the river. There is a stretch on the banks of the Yamuna which is home to elephant keepers who rent out elephants for weddings and events. However, it is really pitiable for the elephants as they bathe in that polluted river water. Japan participates in the Yamuna clean-up project and has installed several filtration facilities, and yet their number is inadequate compared to the demand.

Cleaning the Holy Ganges

Even more serious is the contamination of the holy Ganges. Japan is extending support for this project through the ODA. However, it is not easy to clean the Ganges unless awareness and the civic sense of Indians improve. Making laws to change people's habits is not sufficient.

The Ganges which originates in the Himalayas flows southwards and at Haridwar it changes its course to the east. Upstream of Haridwar there is the holy place, Rishikesh, where the famous English rock band, The Beatles, took part in transcendental meditation courses. Goddess Ganga who is the guardian of the river Ganges is believed to have guided the stream to the earth from the water Lord Shiva had received from the heavens above. She is one of the most popular goddesses in India.

The Ganges is the most sacred river of the Hindus. There is the belief that if you take a dip in it, all your sins till then would be washed away. If a person's mortal remains are immersed in the Ganges, it is believed that it helps the soul liberate itself from the endless cycle of birth and death and achieve emancipation from Karma.

The author visited the Ganges twice. It is clean only till Haridwar as it has a steep flow till that point. Beyond that, it flows eastwards and gradually gets contaminated in the plains by waste water and garbage flowing from factories and homes located along the river.

By the time it reaches Varanasi, the middle of its path in the plains, its colour turns brownish and a large amount of waste can be seen floating in the water. There are many crematorium grounds on the banks of the river in Varanasi. At any given time, several bodies are being cremated in those crematoriums. In the city there are many 'death hotels' (mukti bhawans) where people with terminal diseases or those infirm with age silently wait for their end to come with their families. When they pass away, they are taken to the crematoriums and their ashes are immersed in the river. Even partially burnt bodies of those who cannot afford sufficient volume of wood for cremation are dumped in the river.

The city of Varanasi is concentrated on the left bank, that is, the north side of the Ganges. The north side is regarded as 'this world' and the south side as 'the equinox'. There are virtually no structures on the equinox side. On the northern side there are hundreds of Hindu temples. The roads and lanes are intricate and always full of hustle and bustle.

Mornings in Varanasi is majestic. If you go on the river on a boat from the ghat (a flight of steps leading down to the river), when the red-coloured sun rises from the east side of the river, people clasp their palms and pray to Surya the sun god. During the ancient Graeco–Roman Age, it was believed that Apollo the sun god drove a chariot daily across the sky and disappeared with the sun in the evening and returned next day from the dark with the rising of the sun. Sunrise over the Ganges is also like the sun god returning from the world of darkness.

At the ghats on the riverbank, people rinse their mouths and bathe in the river. There are also people who soak their whole body in the river. Since Hindus are devotees, they believe they are immune to the contamination of the Ganges as faith takes precedence. They believe that if they take a holy dip here, they are absolved of all their past sins. It is a solemn and pious spectacle, but we Japanese somehow cannot do it.

However, the holy Ganges should not be left like this. Goddess Ganga must be angry. Instead of trying to persuade 'devout but environmentally not-so-conscious' Indians by quoting health reasons, it may be more convincing to tell them that the goddess is crying or is angry because of their negligence.

It should be noted here that a good reference for understanding the meaning of Varanasi and the Ganges is the famous work *Deep River* by the Japanese novelist Shusaku Endo.

4.2 JAPAN–INDIA PEOPLE-TO-PEOPLE EXCHANGES FOR THE FUTURE

Delay on people-to-people exchange front
Human resource is the most important aspect in any country, both in nation-building as well as in international relations. Though both the Japanese and Indians are highly capable people, bilateral ties that foster mutual understanding and cooperation are relatively weak. The foremost reason for this state of affairs is that people-to-people exchanges between the two countries are grossly inadequate.

India's population is in excess of 1.38 billion and that of Japan is 126.9 million.

However, the number of Japanese expatriates in India is a meagre 8,655 (October 2015) and that of Indians in Japan is 28,047 (as of December 2015; Foreign Residents Statistics, Ministry of Justice).

Out of over 24 million foreign tourists visiting Japan in FY 2016, the number of Indians visiting Japan was 103,000 (FY 2015) whereas that of Japanese tourists to India was about 210,000 (FY 2015).

Let's compare those figures with China. The total Chinese population was in excess of 1.37 billion, and Japanese expatriates in China numbered 131,161 while Chinese expatriates in Japan were 785,982. Nearly 2.5 million Japanese visit China every year and 4.99 million Chinese tourists visit Japan. (Source is same as that for Indians above).

If we compare the relationship between Japan and India with that between Japan and China, the difference is quite glaring as shown in the table below.

Comparison of Japan–India relationship with Japan–China

	Japan–India	Japan–China	Ratio
No. of Japanese visitors	About 210,000	About 2.5 million	1/12
No. of tourists to Japan	About 103,000	About 2.5 million	1/48
No. of foreign students in Japan	1,102	108,331	1/98
No. of Japanese residents	8,655	131,161	1/15
No. of registered residents in Japan	28,047	785,982	1/28
No. of Japanese language students	About 20,000	About 1.05 million	1/52
Exchange between local governments	13	362	1/28
No. of flights	28/week	690/week	1/25

It is quite obvious from the above data how close geographically Japan and China are (the Chinese call it 'the two countries separated by a narrow strip of water'), how historically there have been deep exchanges, how they have the same race and same characters of language (kanji, though actually it is somewhat different). Compared to this, the gap between Japan and India is quite stark.

The reasons for the above lie on both sides.

Though Southeast Asia emerged as the favourite destination for the majority of Japanese for business and tourism, India still remains distant, psychologically, in addition to the geographical distance. Though the countries west of Myanmar are also parts of Asia, in the perception of some Japanese, they are not really a part of Asia.

On the other hand, Indians are biased towards the West. This may be due to historical and economic reasons as well as the English language being the common factor between them and India. Though Indians are mostly pro-Japanese and have a positive view of Japan, the author has a feeling that highly pragmatic Indians have not given enough importance to Japan; their preference remains the West.

In fact, talking of foreign students, Indian students have normally preferred to study in English-speaking countries such as the US, UK, Canada, or Australia. The objective of foreign students is to get a degree, preferably an MA or PhD. Very few Japanese universities have English as the medium of instruction at the undergraduate level and foreign students need to first learn the Japanese language for around six months to one year. In recent years, some universities have started using the English language as the medium of instruction. Post-retirement, the author worked as a visiting professor at the Graduate School of Asia Pacific Studies, Waseda University. There are two semesters in an academic year. In the first semester, lectures are imparted in Japanese and in the second semester they are delivered in English. However, such cases are exceptional. Generally speaking, Japanese universities are highly inconvenient places for students from overseas, up until now.

Another hurdle for students from overseas is the difficulty in obtaining a PhD degree from a top-notch university in Japan. In the present international society, being a simple graduate is not enough for getting a decent job. If one hopes to succeed in life, he/she has to do a masters degree, or preferably obtain a PhD. Most countries set a greater value on the academic career of an individual. The courses at the undergraduate and graduate levels varies from country to country. However, in the MNCs and international organizations, a degree from an American or a European university carries more weight than from less developed or underdeveloped countries. Indian students who aspire to have a career in an MNC or work in an international organization have less possibility to get such a job if they only have a degree from their native universities. Therefore, they prefer to seek a degree from American or European universities to make their positions secure in the global job market.

Seen differently, the number of students from India in Japanese universities is even less than that from Nepal and Bangladesh. It cannot, therefore, be simply concluded that the problem is entirely on the Japanese side. It could be attributable to the big job-oriented mentality among the Indians.

Investing for the future

The joint declaration issued at the time of PM Modi's visit to Japan in November 2016 stressed the importance of 'investing in people for durable partnership' and an agreement was reached to cooperate on the following fronts.

Hiroshi Hirabayashi

1. In order to strengthen cooperation in tourism, youth exchange, and education, both countries will celebrate the year 2017 as a year of India–Japan friendly exchanges. They will also establish the India–Japan Tourism Council and open an office of the Japan National Tourism Organization (JNTO) in Delhi.

2. The Japanese government will relax visa requirements for Indian students and expand the number of visa application sites for Indian nationals to twenty. (Prior to this, the Indian government also introduced long-term ten-year visas for Japanese tourists and investors and expanded the visa-on-arrival facility.)

3. The Japanese government will provide Indian students with new avenues to avail of scholarships and internship opportunities.

4. The Japanese government will strengthen and expand the SAKURA Science Project (Japan–Asia Youth Exchange Programme in Science) under which young Indian students and researchers visit Japan on the invitation of the Japanese government.

5. Both governments will promote cooperation in sports with a special focus on the Tokyo 2020 (postponed to 2021) Olympics and Paralympics.

6. Both governments will promote interactions between members of parliament and exchanges between local self-governments in both the countries (ties between cities, prefectures, and states).

7. In addition, the joint declaration talks about exchange and promotion in the fields of yoga, empowerment of women, symposium on democracy etc.

4.3 GLOBAL COOPERATION BETWEEN JAPAN AND INDIA

The Japan–India relationship has today grown into one that is decorated with three adjectives namely, 'special', 'strategic', and 'global'. At the summit level as well as the working level, this is always in the minds of both leaders and officials.

The Joint Declaration of November 2016 refers to cooperation between Japan and India in many fields, in particular to the following three points.

1. Working jointly to aid developing nations (triangular cooperation)

Japan and India have decided to combine the human, financial, and technological resources of the two countries to aid third countries in Africa, South Asia; even Iran and Afghanistan have been included as potential recipients of aid. To be more precise, the focus was on triangular cooperation to aid less developed countries.

Triangular cooperation was already in Japan's vision when the author was Director General of the Economic Cooperation Bureau, Ministry of Foreign Affairs. In the beginning, Japan's approach was to aid the countries of Africa that were formerly the colonies of the UK and France with the cooperation of these countries. Japan found collaborating with these countries useful because of their knowledge and experience about Africa. For instance, cooperation to Tanzania (a former British colony) was extended through the aid agencies of Japan and the UK. In the case of East and South African countries, the UK was considered a useful partner, while in the case of West and Central African countries, France was chosen for triangular cooperation.

A similar initiative has now begun between Japan and India. Targeted areas for cooperation between Japan and India will be

East and South Africa, Iran, and Central Asian countries where India has a strong presence and knowledge. Japan's knowledge and personal connections are not deep and adequate enough there, so India's influence and human resources will be put to use for the success of triangular cooperation.

It may appear paradoxical, but the final objective of aid is to eliminate the need for aid. The objective of aid is that the recipient country progresses and eventually 'graduates' from being an ODA recipient country. Thailand is one such case in point. Even if not fully, there are many countries that have graduated from grant aid and receive only yen loans and technical cooperation. These countries that have graduated start extending aid to neighbouring countries. It is the same case with India. Japan is widening the circle of assistance to poorer countries by tying up with such countries.

In addition, in collaboration with the international society, Japan and India are pursuing the development of 'industrial corridors' and 'industry networks' in Asia and Africa.

2. Japan–India cooperation in East Asia

There are several regional groupings in Asia. East Asia has the East Asia Summit (EAS). The ASEAN Summit centred on ASEAN countries (a ten-member grouping consisting of Thailand, Indonesia, the Philippines, Malaysia, Singapore, Brunei, Vietnam, Cambodia, Laos, and Myanmar). There are summit talks between ASEAN member states and countries from outside the region such as Japan, the US, Canada, China, Australia, and India. Japan and India have a broad agreement within the framework of these summits on cooperation to enhance ocean security, fight against terrorism and violent extremism, help cope with climate change and intra-region connectivity (transport and communication networks).

Both India and Japan are concerned about the security situation in Asia. Both have criticized North Korea's nuclear and ballistic missile development activities in the strongest manner and are demanding that North Korea comply with all its international obligations, including the UNSC resolutions and immediately initiate measures towards the denuclearization of the Korean peninsula.

Even with regard to the South China Sea, where some of the Asian nations, including China, make contending claims, both India and Japan have adopted a principled stance that premised on the need to resolve disputes by peaceful means based on the principles of international law, including the United Nations Convention on the Law of the Sea. Both countries want to check and restrain China, which not only has laid claims to the islands in the South China Sea almost in their entirety but also occupies and territorializes them, resorting even to the threat of the use of force.

On the economic front, both Japan and India participated in the East Asia Regional Comprehensive Economic Partnership (RCEP) negotiations. The negotiations started among fifteen countries; ten ASEAN members, Japan, China, Republic of Korea, Australia, New Zealand, and India. Japan and India cooperated with each other and aspired to achieve a 'modern, comprehensive, high quality, and mutually beneficial' agreement. However, India insisted at the last moment to include a clause for freer movement of labour and a less ambitious agreement on tariffs. The other partners objected. In order to prevent China's influence from becoming overwhelming, Japan tried to persuade India to be accommodating, but in vain. Finally, the rest of the negotiating partners decided to conclude the negotiations without India, and signed the protocol on 15 November.

Japan continues to hope that one day India will come back to the RCEP.

On the other hand, twelve countries of the Asia–Pacific region, including Japan and the US, signed the Trans-Pacific Partnership (TPP) Agreement in February 2016 that is broad-based and has greater degree of liberalization not only in the trade of goods, but trade in services, investment, and intellectual property rights.

However, in January 2017, former US President Donald Trump shocked the world by announcing his unilateral decision for the withdrawal of the US from the TPP. The rest of the participants finally abandoned hopes of enacting the original agreement of TPP12 under the Trump administration and opted for a eleven membership TPP (TPP11). Eleven countries agreed to enact TPP11 while leaving the possibility for the eventual participation of the US at a later stage. In December 2018, Mexico, Japan, Singapore, New Zealand, Canada, and Australia enacted TPP11 by ratifying it. In January 2019, Vietnam ratified TPP11 and joined the group. The rest of the signatory countries, Brunei, Malaysia, Peru, and Chile will eventually ratify the agreement. In Japan, TPP11 came into effect from January 2020.

Joe Biden, during his presidential campaign, declared that the US would join TPP11 sometime after his administration commences in January 2021.

China is not a part of the TPP. The TPP is the most advanced comprehensive economic partnership agreement; China cannot fulfil all the conditions of TPP for several reasons such as protection of intellectual property rights (IPR), liberalization of advanced trade, and investment. The TPP is an agreement that can become a model for the whole world to emulate. It is much more advanced than the RCEP.

China is happy that the US withdrew from the TPP and is now trying to take the lead in the RCEP.

Recently China started to show its interest in TPP, maybe to fill the vacuum left by US and to pretend to champion free trade. The US is expected by TPP members, in particular Japan, to come back at the earliest under the Biden administration. The TPP will continue to be a difficult proposition for it so long as India continues to stick to its rigid stance as shown in the RCEP negotiations.

3. Japan and India are comrades in arms for UNSC reform

Even more important is the reform of the international political system. The reform of organizations dealing with international economy such as the IMF and WTO is important, but even more important is the reform of the UNSC.

The UNSC is the most important body of the United Nations. The most important objective of the UN is to secure and maintain international peace and security. To fulfil that responsibility, the UN has the authority to exercise the use of force. However, since the start of the UN, veto power was granted to only five countries, namely, the US, UK, France, Russia, and China (earlier Republic of China and now the People's Republic of China). If one of these countries opposes any decision, the UNSC cannot take action. It is the US and Russia that have used this prerogative most often in the UN's history.

It is over seventy years since the UN was established and yet the system remains the same. Thus, the UNSC has become outdated. It has shown, more often than not, an inability to act on very important issues concerning international peace and security, mainly because of the veto power of its members. Even though the majority of the UNSC members or all the members of the UN itself want to move ahead, one or two permanent members have turned down drafts of resolutions intended to bring positive results. In a way, democracy and legitimacy have been always under a cloud in the actual UN system.

The number of countries that constitute the family of the United Nations has increased today to 196. And, if we include North Korea, that Japan does not recognize, the number is 197. Only four countries, namely, the Vatican, Kosovo, the Cook Islands, and Niue Island are not the members of the UN (as of July 2016). The number of member countries has increased four-fold since the inception of the UN. During this time, there were many countries that had gained power and strength. They are countries like Japan, India, Brazil, and Germany. These four countries are called the Group of Four (G4). Japan is number two in terms of financial contribution to the UN. Except for the US, Japan's financial contribution is bigger than any other permanent member of the UNSC.

Since 2004, the G4 has been campaigning on a large scale for UNSC reform and are aiming to be included in the UNSC as permanent members. The idea of the G4 is to expand and increase the number of permanent members from five to ten, which will include members of the G4 and one representative country from Africa. At the same time, the proposal is to increase the non-permanent member countries by five. Thus, the whole idea is to increase the number of permanent and non-permanent member countries from the present fifteen to twenty-five.

Expanding the UNSC is aimed at a 'democratization' of the UN reflecting the increase in its members and rightfully making the countries that have become qualified as permanent members of the UNSC part of the group.

The UK and France from Europe remain permanent members of the UNSC, but their economies are smaller when compared with that of Japan and Germany. The only difference is that both these countries are nuclear powers whereas Japan and Germany are not. In the present-day world, nuclear powers are not necessarily first-rate countries and non-nuclear second-rate nations. In terms of population, India and Brazil surpass both the UK and France.

As against this, medium-sized countries have formed a Consensus Group (when it started from Columbia, it was initially called the Coffee Group) and are demanding to increase the non-permanent member countries by ten, while opposing the expansion of the permanent members. These countries are aware that they can become non-permanent members but are not qualified to become permanent members. Perhaps their real intention is that they do not want the G4 to further widen the gap with them. Rivals of the G4 have strong hostile feelings against them: South Korea against Japan, Italy against Germany, Pakistan against India, and Mexico against Brazil. Therefore, the Consensus Group is an eyesore for the G4 nations.

Between 2004 and 2005, the prospects of UNSC reform looked bright. But it didn't make much headway after that because of opposition from the Consensus Group as well as strong opposition from the US and China.

For instance, the US is not open to making Brazil and any African country permanent members, let alone giving them veto power. Even today, the US is, at times, criticized and isolated in the UNSC. Except Japan which is pro-America, the US does not feel comfortable increasing the number of permanent members of the UNSC. For the US, it is a nightmare to think of Brazil as a permanent member (as Brazil adopts a tough stance towards the US, at times), and African nations which do not have adequate national power to qualify as permanent members.

China usually pretends to be an ally of developing countries, but since it believes that the permanent membership of the UNSC is a special status, it does not welcome the entry of the G4 into the UNSC. Especially, it does not want Japan to be a permanent member.

The UK and France have shown some understanding of the cause of the G4. These two countries are aware that their power is going to decline in the future. Therefore, they want to have the UNSC reform process resolved before that situation happens, so as to cement their places as permanent members of the UNSC.

In the EU, the chairman of the European Council is the president of EU. International society may want the EU as a permanent member, but not the UK and France. It is for this reason that Germany wants an early resolution to this problem. On the other hand, Italy, which leads the Consensus Group, is afraid that it may be the only country in the G7 that remains out of the permanent membership of the UNSC.

Fifty-three African countries, the largest regional block of the UN, also have their concerns. They are on the whole agreeable to the proposal of the G4. However, there is a bitter contest when it comes to which country from Africa will become the permanent member of the UNSC. In 2004, African countries claimed that two countries should become permanent members of the UNSC. There was also the proposal of the G4 that even if African nations are given the veto power, they should promise not to exercise it voluntarily. However, Africa was bent on having veto power. However, an inability to decide which country should become the permanent member of the UNSC also worked against the whole plan. There were disputes especially between Egypt and Algeria, South Africa, Nigeria, and Kenya.

The G4 is working closely as a team for UNSC reform, and in particular, Japan and India show their teamwork and are in agreement in most situations.

The current stance of the five permanent members of the UNSC on this issue is that the US, UK, and France are agreeable to the entry of Japan and India, while Russia is non-committal. China is non-committal on the surface, and yet will actually oppose the expansion of the permanent members of the UNSC.

By the way, support for Japan's permanent membership is quite strong. It is the second biggest financial contributor to the UN and a pacifist country.

UNSC reform will take place only if two-thirds of the member countries of the UN agree and no permanent member of the UNSC opposes (does not exercise the veto power). Japan will be able to get two-thirds support, but the biggest hurdle will be opposition from China as it may resort to the veto power.

In this way, the path of UNSC reform is not easy. For the successful inclusion of the G4, changing the international situation and increasing pressure from the international society will be much needed. First of all, G4 countries should continue to act in unison and proceed with increased determination.

Seen from this angle, one can understand why continuous consultation and cooperation are regularly needed between Japan and India on this issue.

5

HOW TO LIVE AND WORK IN INDIA

In this chapter, the author would like to introduce the key to understanding Indians based on his information and experience. However, the author's subjectivity may also be included to some extent.

India's geographic size is gigantic. It is a vast country that is nine times the land mass of Japan and almost the same as the size of the EU. It is rich in diversity such as in language, religion, race, local colour and is thus quite profound in all dimensions, which draws many foreigners to it. There are many Japanese who are charmed by yoga, Ayurvedic medicine, Indian dances, and instrumental music. Backpackers come from everywhere to travel in India.

However, as described in this book so far, India has many aspects that are totally different from Japan. There is caste-based discrimination in many spheres of life, a large number of underprivileged people, low literacy rate, unhygienic environment, and underdeveloped infrastructure, to name only a few.

Business persons who interact with Indians can be divided into two categories. They carry contrasting perspectives about India. Those who take a positive view of India find India interesting and worthwhile to interact with, while there are people who do not want to come back here again because of troubles they have encountered during their business interactions. Those who have not experienced India tend to carry a negative image of India based on such stories and rumours.

Some problems are attributable to the Indian side as well. Many Indians have too strong a personality and an attitude of self-assertion. It is because otherwise they would not survive in the highly competitive society in India. Such personality traits can be seen differently by different people who then form their own opinion about the country.

A popular joke that goes around in international society is that in international conferences the toughest task for the chair/moderator is how to handle the Indian and Japanese participants. In case of Japanese, the task is how to make them speak and in case of Indians how to keep them quiet. The longest speech in the General Assembly of the UN was neither by the Soviet Union's Mikhail Gorbachev nor by Cuba's Fidel Castro, but it was by the then Indian defence minister, V. K. Krishna Menon. Menon's speech in 1955, lasting five hours on 23 January, and two hours and forty-eight minutes on 24 January, is to date the longest ever delivered in the United Nations.

5.1 EXTREMES COEXIST IN INDIA AND THE MEAN NUMBERS DO NOT REFLECT THE REALITY

Profound India

India is a 'profound' country. Diverse culture, a long and complex history, rich local colour, jumbled-up yet coexisting religions, nature full of variety from north to south, cultural and historical heritages, animal sanctuaries, widespread spirituality, India has them all.

Many foreigners tend to become repeat travellers attracted by these charms and diversities of India. Many travellers face theft, fraud, or fall ill. Yet they return to India. On the other hand, there are many Japanese who have had unpleasant experiences and do not want to return to India.

The diversity of India in all its dimensions could be bewildering for a foreigner, and yet it is such diversities that also draw foreigners to its soil. Although there may be two clearly defined categories, namely, those who like India and those who dislike India, yet India's attractive force is such that once you interact with it, you cannot remain indifferent.

In the author's subjective observation, 'India is a country of extremes'. Good and bad, right and wrong, wise and stupid, beautiful and ugly, rich and poor, all at the same time in their extreme forms. Wherever you go, you will find coexistence of extremes. In other words, India is a country where the average or the mean value has no meaning. For example, per capita income of India is only a statistical figure and does not lead to correct understanding of the Indian economy. If one compares India to Japan which is a homogenous society, where the gap between the rich and poor is minimal, India may appear to be a difficult country to understand. This is why the Japanese may carry mixed perceptions about India.

Mumbai, the financial capital of India, has the greatest concentration of big businesses such as the Tata Group and Reliance Industries Limited, domestic and overseas financial institutions, and so on. Mukesh Ambani's extravagant multistoreyed-400,000 square feet house stands tall in the heart of Mumbai, one of the world's most expensive addresses. Mukesh Ambani is one of the top ten billionaires in the world.

However, in his neighbourhood there are also slums. There is a huge slum area near Mumbai airport, which offers a shocking spectacle to passengers flying in and out of Mumbai.

5.2 MENTAL PREPAREDNESS FOR INTERACTING WITH INDIANS

Those Japanese who do not like Indians, unfortunately, have perhaps interacted only with the 'bad type of Indians'. If one interacts with a large number of Indians, one realizes that the majority are respectable people. The author, thanks to his occupation, interacted more with such respectable Indians.

Indian expatriates in Japan are also mostly respectable people. The number of foreigners living in Japan or travelling to Japan is on the rise and among them there are some who take to crimes. However, the author has never heard about any Indian having been involved in a crime or in illegal activities in Japan. The majority of them are highly educated, hard-working, and law-abiding people and they help fellow Indians in times of need or distress. Traditionally, they are mostly engaged in trade, finance, and IT. Compared to expatriates from other countries, they are financially better off. In recent years, the number of Indian restaurants is also mushrooming. Both Indian owners and employees are, by and large, honest and hard-working.

Japanese who have lived and conducted business in Southeast Asia are often at a loss to know how to think about India. Since Indians are also Asians, they tend to think that what worked out in Southeast Asia will work in India too, but they tend to be often disappointed (explained in detail later).

Moreover, among Indians whom one meets in international society, such as those working in UN organizations, many have an inflated ego. In search of a new world, Indians escape from India and the intense struggle for survival there and join international organizations. With this survival instinct, many engage in intense competition. There is a need to overcome your rival to succeed in life. Both India and international organizations are places plagued with intense competition. In a competitive world, survival is presaged on upstaging the other.

It is quite understandable that for the majority of Japanese, who have been brought up in a homogenous society stressing the value of harmony, such Indian traits are hard to deal with. However, in the international society, those who are able to successfully live and work in India will have better chances to succeed in any environment in the world.

In view of the above, with what mindset should one interact with Indians? What will ensure success in business? There is no straightforward answer, and yet the author will try to explain based on his observations, requesting readers to fully keep in mind that it could be his 'biased' opinion.

While sympathizing with the harsh environment surrounding Indians, be mentally tough

First of all, one must understand that Indians are struggling for survival in an extremely harsh environment. If possible, one should empathize with the circumstances of the person one is interacting with and at times you may even need to be sympathetic. Ultimately, it is a person-to-person interaction. Understanding or at least trying to understand one's counterpart, empathizing with his or her circumstances and environment, and showing a feeling of empathy is the first step towards enriching one's life and bring about mutual respect and understanding.

India is on the path of achieving rapid economic growth,

but per capita income is still US$1,581 (FY 2015, worldwide survey) and the majority of Indians are poor. Income is low but the living environment is also extremely harsh. Power supply, water, and sewage, all are poor in quality. A comfortable life is the privilege of a limited number of people. Moreover, though unconstitutional and illegal, caste-based discrimination is still strongly prevalent.

One has to be conscious that majority of Indians live and work in such an environment.

Since we rarely travel to remote areas in India, we have to only imagine how Indians live there and how they think. There is a world which is beyond the imagination of most Japanese. Isn't it important and useful to give more than a passing thought to it?

One sees many beggars in the urban areas. Among them, there are quite a few children. When you see them from your car, your heart aches. As soon as the car stops at a traffic signal, children come running and beg. There are times when their parents are also with them. One cannot help sympathizing. One is driven by an urge to do something.

How does one do it? You may feel awkward as a human being, and yet most of the time the answer is 'ignore'. You may close your 'window of conscience' for a while. If you continue to seriously think about it, your nerves will be in tatters. You would be crushed. Even if you give money, it is more often than not taken away by the boss of these beggars. In most cases, a ringleader forms a gang, deploys them at traffic signals in the morning and takes them back again in the evening and collects the money. In the movie *Slumdog Millionaire*, there is a scene in which a leg of a child is broken by an elderly man to cripple him so that he can be used as a beggar in the future. It appears to be a fantasy in the film, but it may be real. Therefore, it may be better to give candy or chocolates to a child. That will directly benefit the child. The problem is that if they do not earn money, their ruthless ringleader will punish them later.

Anyway, one needs to be tough both physically and mentally to live in India.

◆

EXPERIENCES FROM MY DAYS AS A DIPLOMAT (9)

DON'T FORGET THAT INDIANS ARE A PROUD PEOPLE

India is the birthplace of one of the four great civilizations of the world. Both the population and the size of the country are big. India gave birth to religions such as Buddhism, Hinduism, and Sikhism. India also discovered the zero.

Throughout history, there have been many invasions, and it was even colonized. India had to fight hard for its freedom.

Though the fight against invaders and colonial powers is over, India's struggle continues on other fronts. The fight of the Indian people against poverty, caste-based discrimination, and for safeguarding democracy still continues. As a nation, India continues to fight to earn an honourable place in the international society.

Indians are a proud people. They do not give in easily to the great powers. India is trying to become a great power itself. One proof is that while India has received a large amount of yen loans from Japan, as a proud nation it has never defaulted on their repayment.

The author carried out several negotiations with Indians on Japanese ODA especially ministers and senior bureaucrats of the Indian government. They were very friendly, but their attitude was resolute. They maintained negotiations on an equal footing.

The author would like to talk about his own experience on this subject.

At times, a headache for the ambassador was the reluctance on the part of the Indian government to accept grant aid, including emergency assistance.

Whenever a major disaster such as an earthquake or tsunami happens in a developing country, the Japanese government has the established policy to send disaster relief in the form of money and people through cooperation and coordination with the JICA, Japan Red Cross, and NGOs. If necessary, upon request, a team of the SDF is deployed. Developing countries usually welcome such relief in all forms.

However, in the case of India, whether it is human resources or money, it tries to manage by itself to the maximum extent. India does not easily accept disaster relief funds unless it is too big a disaster. It is my belief that India stands out as a proud country, unlike other developing countries.

Once during my tenure, in 2001, the city of Kutch in Gujarat was the epicentre of a major earthquake. The Japanese Red Cross Society dispatched a medical team and JICA also sent one. The Japanese embassy in Delhi sent officials to the site to coordinate. At the devastated site in Kutch, officials slept in the open air till the tents arrived. The author too rushed to the spot by a SDF C-130 transport plane with tents, foodstuff, medicines, and a team of relief personnel. Despite the harsh environment, relief teams and medical corps from many countries set up a makeshift tent village and worked hard.

In this kind of situation, the Indian government declines to accept monetary aid, albeit politely. Not once, but each time any disaster has hit India, the usual reaction was that monetary aid was not accepted since necessary arrangements would be made with its own resources. The Indian government does not compromise in such cases. Whenever the Japanese side insisted, the response was: 'If you still want to help, send the money to the Prime Minister's Relief Fund'. Other countries would immediately accept such aid.

One of the officials of the Prime Minister's Office (PMO) revealed to the author that part of the funds may be misappropriated if the cash is directly sent to the victims or to the local government or organizations. Since it is the Prime Minister's Relief Fund, the PMO will disburse it responsibly and hence 'you can be rest assured about proper usage of your funds'.

Thus, interaction with Indians requires full awareness that they are a very proud people.

♦

Indians' pattern of thinking is similar to western people

We tend to think of Indians as Asians like other Asians. However, Indians' mentality and thought patterns are rather similar to western counterparts.

To put it simply, people in countries close to Japan such as Southeast Asians have a mentality and thought patterns closer to that of the Japanese. Their attitude also, broadly speaking, is soft. Japanese, who have lived in Southeast Asia, may think that Indians also belong to the same category of people, but they are grossly mistaken.

According to the author, it would be correct to think that Indians are a 'much sharper' versions of westerners. The author does not mean that they do not have emotions or sentiments. But they are highly pragmatic and theoretical. They have a strong sense of self-assertion. They are people who live in extremely diverse religious and linguistic environments. India, with a huge population, has competition that is way more intense than that in the West. It is a cut-throat world. Therefore, their self-assertion and attitude to pursue their self-interests are much more intense than that in the West. They zealously protect their interests if they come under attack.

A business deal is done with tough negotiations. Indians do not compromise easily. They would not apologize even if they commit mistakes. Even if an agreement is at times ignored or misconstrued, compensation and payment are resisted until the last minute. Perhaps because the interest rate is high in India, payment or repayment is delayed until it becomes absolutely necessary. The idea is to benefit from the interest by delaying the payment. Therefore, business negotiations should be properly and patiently pursued and before signing a final document, it is necessary to fix the finer details by checking the relevant laws just in case there is a legal dispute in the future. It is needed as a precaution for winning the case in the eventuality that the same has to be adjudicated in a court of law.

Business in India requires time and patience, but it is better to prepare well for it than having to deal with a problematic situation later.

Here the author would like to talk of the three cautions.

First, sufficiently check the creditworthiness of one's counterpart and carry out a detailed due-diligence. Indian business persons are clever and good at striking a deal with international sense and information. It will be a gross mistake to think of India as a normal developing country in this regard. Easy compromise could be a source of future calamity. Some prominent Japanese companies have experienced it the hard way in the past.

It is common for Indians to bargain when doing personal shopping. And it is the same when buying a company. One needs to use one's brain when acquiring a company, buying land, or doing business, but 'guts' are also extremely crucial. After enough preparation, including sufficient research, one needs to have the nerve to withstand hard negotiations.

Second, ensure that one wins the case just in case there is a dispute and the matter goes to a court of law. One may also consider adding a clause to have the International Court of Arbitration in England or Singapore as the place of jurisdiction in the agreement in the event of a dispute. Such dispute management mechanism could help both sides.

In India, court proceedings normally take time, and yet the judicial system is more credible than most developing countries. Especially the Supreme Court is at par with any counterpart in the West. Moreover, lawyers, chartered accountants, and consultants are thorough professionals. Elaborate preparations are needed when entering India and one should be mentally prepared for going to court in the event of a dispute. There are also an increasing number of foreign-owned companies (investment banks, law firms, and certified accounting firms) which have established themselves in the country. It may be worthwhile to invest time and money in trustworthy law and accounting firms. Japanese banks are also present in India. They are well-versed with Indian business affairs.

Besides the Japanese embassy in Delhi, Japan has four consulates—in Mumbai, Chennai, Kolkata, and Bengaluru. The Japan External Trade Organization too has offices in various parts of India and the Japan Bank for International Cooperation also has its office. And then there are the Japanese Chambers of Commerce and Industry comprising Japanese companies and Japanese government institutions in major cities of India. Thus, there are many institutions one can consult with for advice. It may also be useful to learn the keys for success or failure from successful or unsuccessful Japanese ventures in the past.

The Japan–India Association may also provide a useful resource based on its internal and external networks and knowledge about India.

The third is that in case there is an actual dispute, after having discussed the matter well with the counterpart, if no solution is arrived at, one should not refrain from going to a court for arbitration located in a credible country or even to a judicial court in India. Even for Japanese business persons who normally dislike litigation, it is necessary to have mental preparedness for that. Of course, it costs time and money, but one need nerves of steel and the ability to negotiate.

India does not have a dearth of 'top-quality people'

There are many Japanese who complain that India is a difficult country. Especially Indian businessmen and those working in international organizations are viewed as 'sharp', if seen positively and 'cunning', if viewed negatively. It is because they live in a country where survival of the fittest is the principle. However, charming 'top quality' people abound in India. Among the people the author indirectly heard about and directly interacted with, there were quite a few such people.

For instance, the author has encountered or heard of such magnificent Indians including successive Union presidents, some politicians (former prime ministers Nehru, Vajpayee, and Manmohan Singh), upper level courts' (particularly Supreme Court) judges, some IAS and IFS officers, the top brass of the three armed forces, governors nominated by the president, journalists of leading newspapers etc. Even in the business world, there are wonderful people like Ratan Tata, former chairman of the Tata Group. It is the same for university professors and intellectuals.

Indians are well qualified to be active on the international stage with their command over the English language, rational and logical thinking, ability to communicate their opinions persuasively, attitude of self-assertion, bold ideas, and actions.

Indians do not believe in the axiom 'Silence is Golden'. People who do not speak are rather considered to be of no substance or incapable of communicating their thoughts.

Recently in India, graduates from the IITs are more sought after than those from the humanities background. At the end of 2016, there were twenty-three IITs in India. The IIT

Hyderabad is being supported by the Japanese government and the JICA. The IIT is a higher education institution for engineering, but it also has courses in the arts/humanities. There is stiff competition to get into an IIT. There are even preparatory institutes in different parts of the country for IIT aspirants.

Even after successful entry, lectures are quite difficult to follow at IITs and there are students who fail to clear the internal exams. On graduation, those with good results get placement for top jobs in and out of India. In the last few years, the IITs have become well-known throughout the world and graduates with top rankings are rumoured to get a starting salary of about ¥30 million per annum from global companies. Even in the US, especially in the financial and IT industries, there are many IIT graduates leading global companies.

Believe that Indians are pro-Japanese

According to the author's impression, those Indians who have directly or indirectly experienced Japan tend to become pro-Japanese. Comments in the Indian media and internet on Japan are also positive.

The fact that the most important large-scale projects in India such as the metro projects in big cities, the DMIC, freight corridor projects, and shinkansen project connecting Mumbai and Ahmedabad have been entrusted to Japan demonstrates the pro-Japanese stance of Indians and the faith Indians repose in Japanese technology and manufacturing.

Indians may be tough negotiators but it is not because of any mistrust or cautiousness against the Japanese but simply because of business reasons such as: 'How do I make more money with Japanese counterparts?'

In case of any difficulty in business negotiations or at

government offices, it may be worthwhile to point to the extremely cordial history of Japan–India relations and persuade your counterparts that both countries need to work together for the future. To what extent such emotional reference would work depends on the person concerned in the negotiation, but one could at least expect a favourable and considerate response from the Indian side.

◆

EXPERIENCES FROM MY DAYS AS A DIPLOMAT (10)

UNDERSTANDING INDIAN DIVERSITY IS THE STARTING POINT

In order to understand one's counterpart, it is necessary to be fully aware of his/her background. This is true of any country, but since India is rich in diversity, one needs to pay extra attention to it. Though generalization might be inappropriate and prejudice should be avoided, the general perception of Japanese is that Indians in northern India of Aryan background are physically somewhat intimidating while Indians in the south of Dravidian background are perceived to be gentler, which is one of the reasons why Japanese find working with South Indians more comfortable.

SPECIAL ATTENTION TO THE CASTE SYSTEM

The caste system is so pervasive that one needs to understand this in depth in order to understand India more objectively. Partly because it is a unique discriminatory system not to be found in other countries and partly because it is socially and religiously deep-rooted. In many cases it might become necessary to understand that the person one is going to negotiate with or employ belongs to a certain caste. It does not mean changing one's attitude towards that person depending on the caste, but one could make mistakes if one does not know about this aspect.

Japanese live in a homogeneous society where 'everyone is almost equal'. Therefore, most Japanese find the caste system difficult to understand and quite cumbersome to deal with. They tend to find it hard to handle, till they get accustomed to the system.

In Japanese companies located in India, both in offices and factories the notion that 'the premises here are Japanese' prevails and Japanese managers try to persuade Indian employees to follow Japanese norms. On the surface Indian employees of Japanese companies try to follow Japanese norms, yet one should never forget that the customs of the home country are an ever present reality. If a Japanese manager responds wrongly with respect to the caste of an Indian employee, it can become a complicated matter. Therefore, the management of human resources is mostly better entrusted to such Indians who have good knowledge about it and can handle properly caste-based delicate issues when they occur.

The author would like to share his own experience in this regard.

Soon after the author's assumption of office, all the embassy staff gathered in the large hall of the ambassador's residence to welcome the new ambassador and his wife and introduce the staff to them. In the hall, the Japanese staff and local staff stood in a U-shaped formation along the three walls in order of their affiliation. The author and his wife moved in front of each of the staff. The author shook hands with each person and exchanged greetings. Towards the end, there were some Indian staffers who were not prepared to shake hands with the author despite the author having extended his hand. The author then himself dared to stretch and shook hands with them.

The author learnt later that they were Dalits. They have grown up being told not to touch upper-class people. The upper-class people also are not supposed to touch them. Although it is a disgusting word, they are treated as 'untouchable'.

For them, the ambassador was perhaps perceived as belonging to an upper caste. What would have happened, the author wondered, if the author had met the staff in reverse order? Would the upper-class staff have shaken the hands of the ambassador which had touched a Dalit staffer's hands?

The embassy is an extraterritorial place, out-of-bounds for the laws of the recipient country, according to established diplomatic protocols and the

Vienna Convention on Diplomatic Relations. However, it cannot prevent the recipient country's staff from following their practices.

Even if the Japanese staff would tell them that 'since you are in Japanese territory, no caste system is applicable here,' they cannot coerce them into the Japanese way of doing things.

Next morning, the author headed from his residence to his office. It was a one-minute walk. There was a large garden with flowers on the right side of the path that led to the office. Two gardeners were working there and the author spontaneously greeted them by saying 'Namaste'. However, both of them simply looked down at the ground and retreated a few steps. It appeared that these gardeners may have belonged to a lower caste or were Dalits. It was apparently not unusual for Dalits to refrain from meeting the eye of a superior or even responding to a greeting or question. Thereafter, the author made it a point to greet them. As they got used to it, they started returning the greeting quite intimately.

Soon after the author started living in the ambassador's residence, the author requested the Indian staffers who cleaned the floors of the living quarters and the bedroom to also clean the toilet. There were many Indian staff members working at the ambassador's residence. They lived in the servants' quarters (with their families) in a separate building. Their type of work was fixed depending on their occupational category. This staffer whom the author instructed did not say anything directly to him, but called the Dalit staffer who was responsible for cleaning the toilet and ordered him to clean it. The author felt he had made a mistake by asking the person responsible for cleaning the living quarters and bedrooms to clean the toilet as well. He might have felt that he had been treated in a manner that did not befit his caste status.

Within a caste, there are many sub-castes depending on the type of job one is engaged in. The workers are highly aware of such minute differences in job category and deal with them appropriately. On the contrary, if one confuses the issue, it can disrupt the order. Upper-caste members may be left with some ill-feeling. And in the worst-case scenario, they can be nasty to the lower caste person later on.

Hiroshi Hirabayashi

NEED TO BE SENSITIVE TO RELIGION

Some exceptional cases apart, Japanese do not have deep religious faith. Depending on the circumstances, the same person may go to a temple, a Shinto shrine, or even visit a church. In most cases, their faith is superficial.

However, in India, one needs to understand the religious circumstances well. Most Indians are highly pious. They do not visit religious places that are not of their faith, except for sightseeing. There are several cases of communal conflicts in the country, leading at times to riots, between Hindus and Muslims. Though the separation of government and religion is the national policy of India, there are extreme elements on either side who could turn hostile and violent against each other on the slightest provocation.

However, no special care needs to be taken at the workplace with respect to Hindus. Christians and Buddhists also are not so fussy.

However, Muslims are obligated to offer prayers five times a day, praying on their knees. They have to be permitted to go and pray when the prayer time comes. At a factory, they may not be able to go to a mosque to offer prayers, but a prayer room has to be provided for.

Indians love political debate, and yet indulging in religious debate with Indians could be risky and is at best avoided.

BEHIND VEGETARIANISM

It is also necessary to pay attention to food. Not for hygienic reasons, but for the need to pay attention to vegetarianism.

The majority of Indians are vegetarian. The choice of being vegetarian is not dictated mainly by health reasons as is the case with the Japanese. Since it is for religious reasons, one needs to respect it. In short, vegetarians refrain from eating non-vegetarian food, because it is seen as unclean or dirty. This is especially so with the upper-caste Indians.

Originally, this perception was derived from the concept of 'clean/unclean' in Brahmanism and subsequent Hinduism. The doctrine is that human beings must be pure. Buddhism also has the same doctrine. And in Jainism, this concept is implemented more strictly.

The author entertained VIPs quite frequently at the ambassador's residence. At his residence, there was a Japanese chef whom he had recruited from Japan and an Indian chef. Since mainly Japanese food was served at dinners and lunches as well as receptions, the chefs were capable of preparing and serving vegetarian food to Indian guests. Meals were usually buffet style when the embassy organized a big reception in the main hall or the lawn. The author was also invited frequently for dinners and receptions by Indian dignitaries and friends, and it was mostly buffet style. Even if it was a sit-down dinner where seats were fixed for guests, each person went and picked up food that was on display. The chief guest was served by the waiter at his/her table after checking whether the person was vegetarian or non-vegetarian. In the case of a buffet, it is easy for both the host and the guest as the person picks up whatever he/she wants to eat, vegetarian or not.

However, in case of a formal sit-down luncheon or dinner, it is quite cumbersome. Care which is unique to India needed to be kept in mind. It is necessary for both the host as well as the waiters to ensure that food is not wrongly served. Therefore, guests are asked beforehand whether they are vegetarian or non-vegetarian and the seating arrangement is made accordingly. It was ensured by the protocol officers and my wife that waiters would serve the guests correctly by viewing the different colours of chopsticks or chopstick stands arranged in front of each guest on the table according the guest's choice of vegetarian food or non-vegetarian. Waiters were sensitized on it well in advance.

The difference in the degree of vegetarianism and non-vegetarianism from person to person makes it more complicated. Hindus, regardless of being vegetarian or non-vegetarian, do not eat beef. The cow is regarded as a sacred animal and is the vehicle of Lord Shiva. It is called Nandi. In temples enshrining Shiva, a stone statue of Nandi is placed at the entrance to the temple. Due to traffic reasons, now their number in towns have reduced, but some years ago one could find cows sitting in the middle of roads even in a big city like Delhi. Since they are holy cows, no one disturbs them and let them be.

At the ambassador's residence, beef has been served at times. It was because one of the senior government officials well versed with Japan told the author that beef can be served as long as it is Japanese, American, or Australian beef and not the sacred Indian cow. He even asked whether the embassy served Kobe beef. The author replied that with the embassy's budget he can only serve Australian beef.

On the other hand, Muslims do not eat pork. If pork, ham, and sausages are served to them, it will be a big problem. The 'Sepoy Mutiny' described in Chapter 2 is a good case in point.

Even among vegetarians, there are various degrees which make it further complicated. There are flexible vegetarians who don't mind eating egg, while other vegetarians do not eat egg.

Jains are an extreme case. Jains are banned from eating root vegetables (carrot, radish, turnip, potato, sweet potato etc.). According to the author, there may be two reasons behind it. If one eats the root of a root vegetable, the vegetable dies and hence it should not be eaten. Eating leaves and fruits is fine. The second is that when collecting root vegetables, there is a possibility of killing the insects in the soil (such as earthworms). In Jainism, killing any living being is strictly prohibited.

Among the favourite staple dishes of the chef of the residence was seaweed clear soup. However, there are Indians who avoid having soup with seaweed or miso soup. The reason for this is that fish may have come in contact with the seaweed. For them, eating seaweed may amount to eating fish.

Here the author would like to describe about experience of 'clean/ unclean' thinking among the Jains.

The author and his wife were invited many times to weddings of affluent Indians. The wedding of an affluent Indian is an ultra-lavish affair. The lawn of a five-star hotel is leased out and decorated. It is also common that the groom comes to the venue on a heavily decorated horse. A large number of guests are invited. Guests belonging to the upper strata of society are all the more welcome. If you get to know someone through some events or gatherings, you may get invited to a wedding in their family. A Japanese ambassador attending the wedding seemed to bring special dignity and honour for the host.

The wedding reception is usually ostentatious and grand in scale, while the marriage ceremony itself is carried out on a small scale. The wedding rituals take place from around midnight. The holy fire is lit in the middle of a magnificent pavilion set up in one corner of the hall. A number of Brahmin priests camp there and chant Hindu mantras with the bride and the groom sitting in front of them. Selected family members and close friends sit around them. Outsiders like the author can also join and observe the proceedings. Based on instructions from the priests, the bride and bridegroom perform the rituals. With this the marriage is solemnized. During this time, other guests are busy eating, drinking, and chatting.

Once the author was invited to a wedding function held by a rich Jain diamond merchant. It was not in a hotel but under huge tents put up for the purpose. The surprising thing was that all aspects of the reception, from guiding the guests to their seats to serving food and drink were being handled by graceful women clad in gorgeous saris and wearing diamonds. The usual waiters that you find in weddings were missing.

The author was surprised on being told the reason for it. Apparently it would be a dishonour to use the services of low-caste servants for distinguished guests. The author was not sure whether this was the norm in all Jain weddings, but his impression was that the concept of 'clean and unclean' was being thoroughly practised on this occasion.

Another episode is also related to Jains. Once the author was travelling in his car on a rural road and saw a completely naked saint-like person. Literally, he did not have a single thread on his body. Jain and Hindu saints shun everything from money, position, fame, and even family and wander about. This saint was a Jain saint. His mouth was covered with a mask and he had a broom in his hand. The mask was to prevent insects from entering through the mouth or nose. While walking, he swept the ground below with the broom so as not to step on an insect.

However, Jain temples are not in line with such rigid doctrines and are quite gorgeous. They are not colourful and yet they have marvellous and intricate carvings on white marble covering their interiors and exteriors. The author has been to the famous Ranakpur Jain temple in Rajasthan. Many such temples are spread across the states of Rajasthan and Gujarat, and to the south-west of Delhi.

◆

5.3 SIX PS WHICH ARE INDISPENSABLE FOR DOING BUSINESS WITH INDIA

Mr Keiji Nakajima is a long-standing friend of the author and is well-versed with Indian business affairs. He was the chief representative of Sumitomo Corporation when the author was posted here. He has settled down in India post-retirement in order to serve as a bridge between Japan and India. Besides a consulting firm, he operates four restaurants and three hotels in and around Gurugram. He enjoys the trust of both the central government and the Haryana government and is a strong ally of Japanese companies.

Based on his experience in India, Mr Nakajima points to six Ps for succeeding (or not failing) in doing business in India. The author agrees with them and here he would like to introduce Mr Nakajima's views. The six Ps are Product, Price, Place, Person or Partner, Passion, and Patience.

Product and Price

When setting up a factory or selling a product in India, obviously one would need to first think of what to manufacture or what to sell. As seen earlier, the problem is that India has a very broad customer base ranging from the rich to the middle class and the poor. The degree of poverty is also multilayered. Thus, it is necessary to clarify the targeted layer.

For instance, in case, one is targeting the bottom of the pyramid (BOP), costs have to be kept low. One has to factor in the price of the product in line with the volume to be produced or sold. Since India has a large population whose purchasing power may be low, if large volumes are sold among the poor, it will still be commercially viable as the unit cost of the product could come down. It may sell in large numbers at a low profit.

When the author was posted in India, a marketing strategy of Unilever Company of the Netherlands to sell shampoo was the subject of discussion. Unilever initially started selling shampoo like it did in the West. However, the price was beyond the reach of the poor and did not sell well. Those days even the middle class was small in size.

Learning from its failure, Unilever launched shampoo sachets sold at a price of ₹2 each. This was an instant hit. Women from the poor class started buying it. Each sachet was low priced, but the population was 1.2 billion and half of them were women. Men use shampoo as well so the success of the initiative was assured.

Similarly, when Nissin Foods of Japan launched instant noodles at a price of ₹80 per cup, it did not sell well. Then the company did a lot of market research and finally reduced the price, which resulted in an increase in demand. Yakult of Japan has also become popular and its price setting too has been done keeping the Indian consumer's purse in mind. Yakult lady, that is, ladies delivering the product, has become its symbol. Samsung of South Korea expanded its customer base by producing and selling CRT television for the poor. Its strategy was that once their buying power improves, they would buy the higher quality LCD television of Samsung as the brand and product would already be familiar to them.

NTT Docomo of Japan entered into a joint venture with Tata Teleservices Company, a company of the Tata Group, and entered the mobile telephone services business. In the beginning it did well, because unlike the practice of billing per minute, it introduced per second billing. This became an instant hit and subscribers increased rapidly. It was a good start for the joint venture. Its customers belonged to the class that could afford a mobile phone, though they were not from the BOP. The concept was the same. However, the competition matched the billing within no time. NTT Docomo decided to break the joint venture. There were other reasons also such as permissions not being granted to the joint venture in the metropolitan cities. Ultimately NTT Docomo retreated from the Indian market.

As for electrical appliances, it is necessary to take into consideration the climate (hot weather) and power situation (power breakdown and voltage fluctuation etc.) in India. The author has heard that Nokia of Finland was initially successful because it provided a torch in mobile phones. Mobile phones could be used as a torch in case of sudden power failure. Toshiba sells a PC that has a battery and semiconductor that can withstand power breakdowns and voltage fluctuation.

In India, families belonging to the middle class and above have multiple servants at home. Because of the caste system, work is strictly divided among them. Fortunately, the manpower cost is extremely low. However, theft and cheating is sometimes a problem. Therefore, one home appliance manufacturer launched a refrigerator with a lock. It is a simple solution but quite an effective one.

In India, the author felt the significance of the old saying 'When in Rome, do as the Romans do', namely, slash prices and compete on volumes.

Person or Partner (business counterpart or partner)

Japanese are not familiar with India and hence it is a difficult market and society for them. Therefore, generally speaking, Japanese need a local partner to set up a factory or offer goods or services here. Entering into India has become much easier compared to earlier times. The central government as well as state governments have taken many proactive steps to attract foreign companies, especially Japanese companies to India. These steps include the establishment of a single window for Japanese investment, constructing industrial townships dedicated to Japanese companies, and relaxation of regulations that used to hamper entry of companies etc. Through the good offices of PM Modi, a team called 'Japan Plus' has been constituted exclusively for Japanese companies in the Ministry of Commerce and Industry. It is manned by a Japanese expert who is well-versed with Indian business affairs.

However, India is after all India. The plethora of regulations remains and bureaucrats' mindsets have not changed completely. Even Indians complain of regulations and the red tape of politicians and bureaucrats. Bribes are demanded explicitly or implicitly. Here, the saviour of the Japanese company is the Indian partner. In addition, he can also do 'tricky' jobs that need to be done with respect to government officials. Offering a bribe is today an international crime based on the rules of the Organisation for Economic Co-operation and Development (OECD) and even if it has been paid overseas, criminal prosecution for the same can be done in Japan. In this regard it can be a risky proposition, if the Japanese expatriate thinks 'When in Rome do as the Romans do'. A partner who can give suitable advice or deal with such situations comes quite handy.

When one is accustomed to the market, labour environment, and method of dealing with government officials, it becomes easy to manage one's business.

Suzuki Company, that has been operating its automobile business for long in joint venture with India, has set up its latest factory in Gujarat, independently without any Indian partner. Honda's joint venture for its two-wheeler business in India that was already successful when the author was posted in India was called off and today the company is running its two-wheeler business all by itself. Its joint venture partner was a small-sized family group from Delhi and it was assumed that it could not match Honda.

Generally speaking, Indian companies are mostly run as family businesses. They continue to be that way even if the size becomes big such as the Tata Group. It is similar to South Korea's Samsung and Lotte. A joint venture with a small business is fine at the initial stage. However, it runs out of steam when the joint venture wants to infuse more capital and accelerate growth. If the equity ratio is maintained at the same level between partners, a large amount of funds is required. If not so, the equity ratio of the partner declines and so does his say in company matters. Thus, the Indian partner who was earlier dependable starts becoming a fetter in the growth of the company. Kirloskar, the partner of Toyota, is a mid-size group of Mumbai and has kept pace with the requirements of Toyota quite well.

In short, the entry into India of a Japanese company and its success are determined to a large extent by the partner. On the other hand, the person on the Japanese side is also important.

Indian business style is, by and large, top-down. In quite a few instances, it is also affected by the caste system. Just the way caste often impacts the business environment in

India so also does it do so when a foreign partner is involved. Moreover, the speed with which to do things in India is faster than that in Japan, and most of the times speedy decision-making is needed.

Therefore, the top management, that is, chairman and president in the head office, need to be sufficiently involved in the India business. When entering India, a round of meetings and discussions with the concerned officials of the central government ministries is usually indispensable. The concerned agencies are the Ministry of Commerce and Industry, the Ministry of Finance in case of finance related business, ministries in charge of various business categories and in case of very big projects, even the Prime Minister's Office. In addition, top officials of each state (chief minister, minister of commerce and industry at the state level, state secretary of commerce and industry, and the state industrial development and investment corporation) must absolutely be engaged. Therefore, it is important for the top management of Japanese companies to visit India and explain the corporate strategy and positioning of the India business and build a relationship of trust with the Indian side.

Suzuki was successful because Chairman Osamu Suzuki himself took the lead. He met successive prime ministers starting with Mrs Indira Gandhi and made efforts to form a strong base in India by engaging himself to deal with important decisions. The author has always advised the top management of Japanese companies during his ambassadorship and even now as president of the JIA to visit India and develop connections with the political circles in India and build a relationship with the top management of the counterpart company.

In recent times, Mr Masayoshi Son, Chairman and CEO of SoftBank Group made an unannounced visit soon after PM

Modi assumed office. He met PM Modi personally to impress upon him his proactive stance towards India.

In the last few years, the interest of the top management of Japanese companies in India has grown and the author is glad that they have started travelling to India on their own initiative.

However, perhaps because of the low priority given to India over, say, Southeast Asia, there are still many Japanese companies in which the India business is entirely left to the lower level of executives. Many Japanese expatriates in India express their dissatisfaction and vent their frustration about the lack of understanding about India among their top and senior management in the head offices.

Recently, some leading trading houses and manufacturing companies of Japan have appointed chief representatives of the local subsidiaries in India—these individuals have the status or rank of director of the board or executive officer in the respective head offices in Japan. They can take decisions locally and quickly without having to ask the head office each time.

There are many executives of Japanese companies who do not speak English. And it is also a fact that the English spoken by Indians is difficult to understand. Many Indians who speak English with foreigners speak too fast with what is called a Hindi accent. There are many foreigners who jokingly call it 'Hinglish'.

However, since Indians speak with confidence, foreigners try to listen carefully to Indian interlocutors. On the other hand, since Indians live in a multilingual society, they have the capability to understand English spoken by foreigners; they are also able to learn other languages quickly.

According to the author's experience, there are very few interpreters for Japanese language who can correctly interpret complicated business negotiations. Often, not only are they unable to communicate the intent of the Japanese side, at times, they even cause misunderstandings and end up offending the counterpart. Business interpretation is different from interpretation for the purposes of tourism. It is a must to make the interpreter study the content and nature of the business to be discussed and gain information about the proposed partner companies in advance. In this regard, it is preferable to use an internal person within the company who has enough information and experience than using an external interpreter.

Luckily, there are an increasing number of Japanese business persons who have experience of working in India and are ready to return to India to help Japanese companies as a post-retirement job.

Place

India is big and diverse. The business environment, economic development, especially infrastructure development, stance of the state governments for attracting foreign companies, stability of the state governments etc., vary from place to place.

As of October 2016, there were 1,305 Japanese companies and 4,590 business establishments across India. These Japanese companies were concentrated in the National Capital Region to the southwest and south of India.

From Delhi NCR towards the southwest, they were located in the region extending from Haryana, Rajasthan, Gujarat, Maharashtra and further south-east down to Karnataka and Tamil Nadu to its east, referred to as the 'arc'.

Some of these metropolises and suburbs can be categorized as suitable venues for the entry of manufacturing and service industries like IT etc. Andhra Pradesh and Telangana (which was a part of Andhra Pradesh until recently) are also qualified as the right place to enter.

There are many industrial and commercial units located in West Bengal in eastern India centred around Kolkata. However, in the balance half of eastern India, there are virtually no Japanese or foreign companies. It is quite natural for iron and steel and coal and coke plants to be located in Bihar and Jharkhand that have raw material deposits.

However, compared to the above-mentioned arc, these places are quite undeveloped. It would be better not to have high expectations of companies located in these areas. Japanese companies that enter these places often need to build captive power generation, water and sewage facilities, and access roads by themselves.

To the contrary, entry in one of the industrial townships, especially townships constructed mainly for Japanese businesses, is recommended as the necessary infrastructure is already developed to a great extent and local authorities are more hospitable. There exist such townships in many locations along the 'arc'.

Let me draw the attention of readers to the following well-known story. Tata Motors of the Tata Group firmed up the concept of a small car called 'Nano', a people's car for Indians in 2003. Since it was to be priced at ₹100,000, it was also called the 'One lakh car'. 'Nano' means 'one billionth of the stated unit'. In short, it means 'extremely small'. Ratan Tata, Chairman of the Tata Group, decided to adopt it as the name for his small car.

Tata Motors bought land from farmers in Singur in West Bengal. However, Mamata Banerjee, the powerful leader of the All India Trinamool Congress party, which was an opposition party then, questioned the land acquisition and launched a powerful movement to oppose it. Tata Motors was at last forced to abandon the project as there was uncertainty about its future viability. Seeing this situation, Narendra Modi, the chief minister of Gujarat, then threw a lifeline to Tata Motors. Since his chief ministership days, he has been proactive in attracting foreign companies and had established 'Vibrant Gujarat', a large-scale trade exhibition-cum-investment summit in Gujarat. Modi immediately offered state-owned land in Sanand in Gujarat to Tata Motors. Owing to the state government's support, Tata's Nano plant was completed in just one year. It became operational from June 2010.

This anecdote came to be widely known not only in India but also internationally, as reflecting the fate of a project depending on its location in India. Indeed, it underlined the importance of selecting the right place for any investment project.

The author visited Kolkata in March 2017 and along with the Japanese Consul General Masayuki Taga called on Mr Amit Mitra, Finance and Commerce and Industry Minister of West Bengal. The author found that things had changed a lot in Kolkata since he had interacted with Mr Mitra when the latter had been the secretary general of the Federation of Indian Chambers of Commerce & Industry (FICCI) in Delhi. He is one of the 'respectable Indians' that the author earlier wrote about. While discussing the matter with him, the author learnt that the state government is quite proactive in supporting foreign companies, especially Japanese companies, and the Tata Motors episode appeared to be a matter of the distant past. The investment climate of West Bengal is undergoing change with time.

Passion and Patience

India being a difficult place in several respects, the last Ps are Passion and Patience. However, since it is a form of spiritualism, no explanation is needed.

Mr Nakajima has since then been talking of his business theory based on tens of Ps which are described in detail in his Japanese book, *Chronicle of 40 Years of Battle of India Business.*

◆

JAPANESE COMPANIES IN INDIA (AS OF OCTOBER 2016)
(1,305 COMPANIES, 4,590 BUSINESS ESTABLISHMENTS)
NCR, NORTH, NORTHEAST INDIA: 1,585 BUSINESS ESTABLISHMENTS
DELHI: 323 BUSINESS ESTABLISHMENTS

Distributors of manufacturers, trading companies, finance, liaison offices etc. Highly convenient due to location of administrative organizations, Japanese school, direct flights etc.

HARYANA AND RAJASTHAN: 935 BUSINESS ESTABLISHMENTS

Factories and distributors of Suzuki, Honda (two-wheelers), Panasonic, Daikin, automotive parts manufacturers, Nihon Densan, machine trading companies, consumer durables etc., are located here. These states are close to Delhi, highly urbanized and working and living environment is good.

UTTAR PRADESH: 309 BUSINESS ESTABLISHMENTS

Honda (four-wheeler), Yamaha, Sumitomo Electric, automotive parts manufacturers etc. New entrants are fewer due to lack of land availability and delay in development of housing environment. It is the satellite area of Delhi and many group housing societies and IT companies are concentrated here.

WEST INDIA: 1,163 BUSINESS ESTABLISHMENTS
GUJARAT: 300 BUSINESS ESTABLISHMENTS

TOTO, Hitachi Hi-Rel Electronics, Suzuki, Honda etc. There is a concentration of chemical and automobile companies here. Infrastructure development is the most advanced and the state is also developing as a base for exports.

MAHARASHTRA: 709 BUSINESS ESTABLISHMENTS

In Mumbai, NYK, Yamatake, Toyo Engineering, trading companies, finance, shipping, pharmaceuticals, consumer durables companies, etc., are entering one after another.

In Pune, Ebara, Sharp, Keihin, Yazaki, Bridgestone, automotive parts, etc., are located here. Japanese companies are small in number but there are many local and western companies concentrated here.

EAST INDIA: 385 BUSINESS ESTABLISHMENTS
WEST BENGAL INCLUDING KOLKATA: 193 BUSINESS ESTABLISHMENTS

Dainippon Ink and Chemicals, Kubota, Hitachi Construction Machinery, Iron and Steel, trading companies etc., are located here. It is a comparatively poor and underdeveloped region and the concentration of industries other than resource raw materials industries is small. However, the population of the region is in excess of 300 million and has good prospects in the future.

SOUTH INDIA (KARNATAKA): 476 BUSINESS ESTABLISHMENTS
KARNATAKA (BENGALURU AND ITS VICINITY): 476 BUSINESS ESTABLISHMENTS

Toyota. Komatsu, Fanuc, Nissin Foods, Citizen, machine tools, semiconductors, IT, automotive parts etc., are to be found here. It is famous as the Silicon Valley of India and it has a concentration of hi-tech and machinery industries. It has high altitude and good weather and is called the most livable city in India.

SOUTH INDIA (EXCLUDING KARNATAKA): 981 BUSINESS
ESTABLISHMENTS
TAMIL NADU: 582 BUSINESS ESTABLISHMENTS
TELANGANA AND ANDHRA PRADESH: 104 BUSINESS
ESTABLISHMENTS

Nissan, Yamaha, Ajinomoto, Toshiba, Hitachi-Aloka Medical, Komatsu, Kobelco
Construction Equipment, Isuzu, Unicharm, Eizai, machinery trading companies,
automotive parts etc., are located here. New manufacturing companies
are entering this area because it has one of the few trading ports in India,
a good number of engineering colleges, and a concentration of automobile
manufacturers. Due to rapid growth, inadequacy of infrastructure has been
exposed.

(Source: Prepared based on material provided by the Ministry of Foreign
Affairs, Japan).

EPILOGUE & ACKNOWLEDGEMENTS

Books published in Japan so far on India–Japan relations have invariably focused on some specific aspects of India—Indian philosophy, Buddhism, history etc. Books coming out from Japanese universities were mostly from the faculties (departments) of literature. More recently, there has been a diversification and fields such as Indian economy, business, and diplomacy have been covered. Books written by Indians who have lived in Japan, on Indian society and business affairs, are additions to the existing literature on India–Japan relations. In more recent times, television programmes and other mass media have started to show increased interest in, and disseminate information on, India and bilateral issues. However, in the author's view, these books, articles, and programmes capture only one or few dimensions of the complex Indian society.

Therefore, the author has consciously tried to make this book different from those written so far. With a view to do so, he has been led by two considerations.

First, the author has tried to give a bird's eye view of India as a whole. Holistic perspective in mind, he has dared to touch upon India's history, society, religion, culture, economy, politics, diplomacy, and security as well as Japan–India relations. The time frame extends from the historical view of

India to the contemporary 'Japan–India special strategic global partnership'. As a result, readers may find it inadequate if they are looking for an in-depth analysis of India and Japan–India relations.

Secondly, the author has tried to present in a candid manner his experiences and knowledge acquired through his long association with India of fifteen years as the Japanese ambassador in India and as the President of the Japan–India Association thereafter. He has consciously tried to write what others cannot or often overlook. He has portrayed facts as they are, while with regard to evaluation and observation on various Indian aspects, he has dared to put even subjective ones in front of readers.

The five years when the author was posted in India saw some stormy and tumultuous events.

Within two months of his assuming office, he received the intense 'baptism' of nuclear tests by India, which plunged India–Japan ties to its nadir and posed a peculiar diplomatic challenge to him as the ambassador of Japan. He also experienced a critical moment in 2002 when India and Pakistan were almost on the verge of a war. The author though is the type who gets an adrenaline rush when he is confronted with a challenging situation. He could overcome all those challenges thanks to the cooperation of his colleagues at the embassy.

Then came the time when bilateral ties needed to be restored after the nuclear hiccup. This happened when the author's request was accepted by PM Yoshiro Mori for the path-breaking visit to India in August 2000. This historic visit resuscitated the flagging relations between the two countries with the establishment of the 'Japan–India Global Partnership'. Not only was the crisis created by the nuclear tests overcome, the visit laid the very foundation for the present-day Japan–India relationship. The author could also solemnize a series of events related with the fiftieth anniversary of the establishment of diplomatic relations between Japan and India in 2002.

India is a country which presents big differences between what you have heard and what you actually see. Moreover, in order to know this vast country with immense diversity, it is inadequate to just visit Delhi or the metropolitan cities. India's depth, diversity, and historical weight can be understood only when one gets an insight about the real India by visiting rural India in person. Impressions formed from one's experience in metros about India would be flawed unless one sees the width and breadth of India in various states and observes closely the kind of life and customs people follow.

The author visited twenty of the twenty-eight states of India (as of 2019). If one visits remote areas, one can get in touch with innumerable aspects of the country's historical, religious, and cultural heritage that cannot be covered in a life in Delhi. India is endowed with innumerable sites of attraction to visit, among them thirty-four UNESCO World Heritage Sites, as of 2016.

The author recommends that Japanese readers of this book travel to India. In recent years, package tours organized by first-rate travel agents have increased and one can travel in India with peace of mind. India's UNESCO World Heritage Sites are essentially cultural heritage sites that have high historical value, and yet there abounds rich natural heritage too. The visit to Buddhist and Hindu holy places, the author promises, will be an eye-opener and there is even a possibility that the visitor's view of life might change due to the exposure to a different culture.

As for the Hindu holy places, the foremost is Varanasi where the sacred Ganges flows. Visiting Varanasi and Khajuraho, which are often presented in the same package tour might change the visitor's way of thinking about life.

The Buddhist holy place of Sarnath is in the suburbs of Varanasi. Not just the places where Buddha lived such as Bodh Gaya and Sarnath, Buddhist heritage sites spread all over India such as the Ajanta caves should prove to be places of unfailing interest for the Japanese. Two Bodhisattva images on the murals in the first cave of Ajanta resemble the images on the murals of the Golden Pavilion of the Horyuji Temple, a UNESCO World Heritage Site, and the oldest wooden temple in the world in Nara. They came from India to Japan through the Silk Road.

By the way, the paved road to Ajanta from Aurangabad was constructed with a Japanese yen loan. Japan has also extended state-of-the-art technical cooperation for the conservation of the Ajanta caves which are threatened by air and water pollution.

Many palaces of the maharajas scattered over the state of Rajasthan are available for tourists as tourist sites and even hotels. For example, Lake Palace in Udaipur in Rajasthan is a dream-like palace. Though somewhat expensive, the Palace on Wheels, the so-called Maharaja Express, that starts from Delhi and takes tourists to places of historic interest in Rajasthan over the course of one week, is a luxury train even better than the Orient Express. The author guarantees that the visitor will get a royal feel while travelling by this train.

Nature is also rich and changes from North to South. From the Himalayas covered with perpetual snow to tropical beaches having plenty of palm trees and to the holy place of Kanyakumari (Cape Comorin) on the southernmost tip, touristic charms abound wherever one goes. For animal lovers, there are national sanctuaries with tigers, lions, elephants, and rhinos all over India. It is the world of *The Jungle Book*.

Indians that the author has interacted with have invariably been friendly to the Japanese people. Not only at ambassador's official functions but the author's interactions with Indians on the personal level have always been a pleasant experience.

The author always praised the Indian staff for the good management of the embassy. They were always friendly and respectful towards him. But he could not escape from being cheated once by the driver of his personal car and, another time, by one of the servants at his residence. Thus, he could share his bitter experience with other Japanese expatriates living and working in less privileged environments.

The number of expatriates those days was small compared to today. Still, they devoted themselves to work despite facing hardships in day-to-day life and at work. Perhaps because of this reason, there is strong solidarity among the Japanese expatriates in India. The author and his wife tried to mingle with them both at the official and personal level. The idea was to give them a feeling that the Japanese government is always with them. In return, they also gave us the immense pleasure of their company and a sense of mutual trust. Since the official residence of the ambassador is quite large and splendid, the author tried to make the best use of it by organizing a large number of diplomatic and cultural programmes to the maximum extent. The embassy was always sensitive about security, and yet the author made his official residence accessible to the expatriates as well as to Indian dignitaries. Even today, Japanese who were posted in India, whether they be diplomats, business persons, journalists, or scholars, hold their alumni meetings on a regular basis in Japan to recall their happy or not-so-happy experiences. There are three alumni associations in existence depending on when their members were posted in India.

In this book, the author has tried to describe India from diversified perspectives transcending time and space. Maybe it was too ambitious in its attempt. There could also be some factual errors.

As the title suggests, India is on the path to superpower status after the US, China, and Russia. Although several countries may become major powers in future, after India, there may not be any other country that will have 'super' prefixed to its name. Hence, India will be the 'Last Superpower'.

Such an India is a 'super' friendly nation to Japan. In this book, the author has tried to do his best to present a 'comprehensive' and 'encompassing' understanding of India that assumes increased importance for Japan as well as the international society.

This book would not have seen the light of the day without the encouragement and cooperation of a large number of people. My special gratitude goes to: Mr Takashi Nagasaki of Nikkei BP responsible for editing this book; Gurugram-based Mr Keiji Nakajima, who is an authority on India's businesses; Japanese businessman Mr Ryuko Hira (original Indian name is Kamlesh Punjabi) naturalized in Japan some fifty years ago who is contributing to the Japan–India relationship in a big way and to the author's colleagues at the Japan–India Association. Three distinguished stalwarts, namely Chairman Osamu Suzuki of Suzuki Company, Dr Sengaku Mayeda, Professor Emeritus at the University of Tokyo, and Mr Soichiro Tahara, distinguished journalist and opinion leader, recommended this book to the public. They too deserve special thanks from the author.

Hiroshi Hirabayashi

This English edition was made possible by Mr Deepak Vasdev and his son, Anirudh, who with their deep friendship and respect for me have taken initiative and made tremendous efforts to choose a translator—Professor Prem Motwani, eminent Japanologist from Jawaharlal Nehru University, and publisher Aleph Book Company. The publication would not have been possible without the support of my Indian friends who showed heartfelt sympathy and generosity, especially Zeus Law Firm, Lipidata Systems Ltd, Fujitsu Frontech Ltd, India, and DCM Shriram Industries Ltd.

And last but not least, the author would like to thank his wife, Kimiyo, because she not only supported him and shared both pleasure and hardship during their stay in India but also made appropriate and even scathing criticism on the manuscript during the writing of this book.

Hiroshi Hirabayashi
Tokyo
January 2021